THE CHRISTIAN ALTAR

AN ANGLO-SAXON ALTAR

This picture from the Benedictional of St. Ethelwold was made at Winchester about A.D. 980. The altar stands under a ciborium and is enveloped in a silk pall of violet on which stand only a chalice and paten. The bishop stands on the nave side of the altar from which he has turned to give the episcopal blessing before the Communion. The altar has neither reliquary nor reredos; but the celebrant does not celebrate *versus populum* since Anglo-Saxon churches were usually orientated.

The scene may represent St. Ethelwold at the consecration Mass of Winchester Cathedral in A.D. 980.

THE
CHRISTIAN
ALTAR

In History and Today

BY

CYRIL E. POCKNEE

LONDON

A. R. MOWBRAY & Co. LIMITED

First published in 1963

PRINTED IN GREAT BRITAIN BY
A. R. MOWBRAY & CO. LIMITED IN THE CITY OF OXFORD
2662

Preface

THE last half-century has witnessed an intense and growing interest in the origins and development of Christian worship, both in rite and ceremonial; and there have been many works dealing with the liturgy in most of its aspects. Yet it is true to state that there exists no full-scale study in English of the historical development of the Christian altar. Students and scholars have had to rely on an essay by the late Edmund Bishop, first published in the *Downside Review*, in July 1905, under the title, 'On the Christian Altar', which in spite of its many excellencies is too limited in its scope. The two great volumes, *Der christliche Altar*, of Father Joseph Braun, S.J., published in 1924, have not received the attention amongst English-speaking Christians which they deserve. I hope the many references I have made to that work will testify how much I am indebted to them. Likewise I hope it will be obvious how much I owe to the late Michel Andrieu, whose works I have cited in many places. Lest it should be thought that I have relied solely on Roman Catholic authorities I would add my indebtedness to our own Joseph Bingham's *Origines Ecclesiasticae*, which, although written in the first half of the eighteenth century, is still a mine of information.

The manuscript of this work was read by Dr. F. Brittain and Dr. F. J. E. Raby of Jesus College, Cambridge, and the Reverend Richard Tatlock. I am indebted to them for their advice and criticisms on a number of issues. They are not, however, responsible for the final form of the text and any blemishes which remain. I am indebted to Messrs. Sands & Co. of King Street, London, W.C.2, for their kind permission to use parts of pages 108–110 of the English version of Salaville's *Introduction to the Study of the Eastern Liturgies*.

I write as an Anglican priest; but I hope this work may be acceptable in some degree to all who celebrate and observe the Sacrament of the Altar in obedience to their Lord's command since that Sacrament should also be one of unity and fellowship in Him.

CYRIL E. POCKNEE.

TWICKENHAM
Advent, 1962

List of Contents

		PAGE
INTRODUCTION	. . . . . .	13
Plates 1–16	. . . . .	17
1. THE LORD'S TABLE	. . . . .	33
2. SIDE ALTARS AND THEIR MULTIPLICATION	. .	51
3. THE ALTAR CANOPY AND ITS VEILS	. .	55
4. ALTAR SCREENS	. . . . . .	64
Plates 17–32	. . . . .	65
5. ORIENTATION AT PRAYER AND THE POSITION OF THE CELEBRANT AT THE ALTAR	. . .	88
Plates 33–34	. . . . .	97
6. THE HANGING PYX	. . . . .	101
7. SOME PRACTICAL CONSIDERATIONS IN THE DESIGN OF AN ALTAR	. . . . . .	106
APPENDIX	. . . . .	108
SELECT BIBLIOGRAPHY	. . . .	109
INDEX	. . . .	111

List of Illustrations

PLATE   PAGE

AN ANGLO-SAXON ALTAR: From the Benedictional of St. Ethelwold, tenth century . . . *Frontispiece*

1. A BASILICAN ALTAR WITHOUT A CONFESSIO: Castel Sant' Elia, Nepi, Italy 17

2. ALTAR WITH A CONFESSIO: Anagni Cathedral, Central Italy 18

3. CIBORIUM WITH REREDOS: Sant' Apollinare in Classe, Ravenna 19

4. A GERMAN SUPER-ALTAR: Twelfth century . . 20

5. A PRECIOUS METAL FRONTAL: Altar in the Church of St. Ambrose, Milan 21

6. A SPANISH TESTER: Thirteenth-century canopy in Episcopal Museum, Vich, Spain 22

7. A MEDIEVAL ALTAR WITH CANOPY: High Altar, Gerona Cathedral, Spain 23

8. THE CHAPEL OF HENRY VII, WESTMINSTER: Restoration of sixteenth-century canopy in 1935 . . . 24

9. A RENAISSANCE ALTAR: From a fresco in the Piccolomini Library, Siena, by Pinturicchio, 1498 . . . 25

10. AN ENGLISH BAROQUE CANOPY: St. Mary Woolnoth, London, 1727 26

11. (*a*) AN ENGLISH MEDIEVAL TESTER: Clun, Salop, fifteenth century 27

    (*b*) THE CANOPY IN NORWAY: Hopperstad Church, mid-twelfth century 27

12. OLD ST. PETER'S, ROME: From a fresco, Vatican, *circa* 1520. 28

13. (*a*) THE SCREEN IN THE EAST: From Rohault de Fleury, *La Messe*, Tome III, Plate 241 29

    (*b*) AN EARLY BYZANTINE SCREEN: Fifth-century screen and altar, Byzantine Museum, Athens . . 29

14. TRIPTYCH AND RELIQUARY: Thirteenth-century portable triptych, School of the Meuse . . . 30

15. A CHASSE OR PORTABLE RELIQUARY: Thirteenth-century French enamel on copper-gilt 31

16. THE MASS OF ST. GILES: Flemish painting, 1500, by the Master of St. Giles. (National Gallery, London) . 32

17. THE APOGEE OF ITALIAN BAROQUE: Altar of St. Ignatius Loyola 65

18. AN ENGLISH MEDIEVAL REREDOS: Fourteenth century, East Anglian School, Norwich Cathedral . . . 66

19. THE SYRIAN LITURGICAL PLAN: From Lassus and Tchalenko, *Ambons Syriens*, 1950 . . . 67

20. A GERMAN TRIPTYCH: Sixteenth century, North Germany 68

21. A RUSSIAN ICONOSTASIS: Chapel of the Institute of Orthodox Theology, Paris 69

22. FOUR MEDIEVAL PYXES: Thirteenth-century Limoges enamel 70

23. AN ENGLISH PYX-CLOTH: Hessett Church, Suffolk . . 71

24. A FRENCH RENAISSANCE ALTAR: From the *Caerimoniale Parisiense*, 1703 72

25. A SPANISH HANGING PYX: From an illustration in MS. 9169, F. 20v., Bibliothèque Royale, Brussels . . 73

26. A EUCHARISTIC DOVE: Salzburg Cathedral, twelfth century 74

27. A SPANISH PYX: Sixteenth century, silver parcel-gilt . 75

28. TERRACINA CATHEDRAL, ITALY: Twelfth century . 76

29. MODERN ROMAN CATHOLIC ALTARS: Church of Our Lady of Peace, Braintree, Essex, designed by Geoffrey Webb . 77

30. CONTEMPORARY AND LITURGICAL: Altar of St. Katherine, Hammersmith, by Colin Shewring, 1961 . . 78

31. A RIDDEL POST ALTAR: Tring Parish Church, Hertfordshire, designed by the late F. E. Howard . . 79

32. THE LITURGICAL ALTAR: Cathedral Church of St. Andrew, Aberdeen, by the late Sir Ninian Comper, 1940 . 80

33. A MODERN ORTHODOX ALTAR: The Sanctuary and Altar of the Metropolitan Cathedral at Athens . . 97

34. A THROW-OVER FRONTAL: American War Memorial Chapel, St. Paul's Cathedral, London . . . 98

ACKNOWLEDGEMENTS

PERMISSION to reproduce the following illustrations is acknowledged:

Frontispiece—The British Museum.

Plates 1 and 2—Mansell-Alinari.

Plates 4, 14, 15 and 29—Victoria and Albert Museum, London.

Plates 6 and 7—Ampliaciones Y Reproducciones Mas, Barcelona.

Plate 8—The Dean and Chapter of Westminster.

Plate 11 (*a*)—National Buildings Record, London.

Plate 16—The National Gallery, London.

Plate 18—E. P. Le Grice, Norwich.

Plate 23—The British Museum, London.

Plate 25—Bibliothèque Royale, Brussels.

Plate 26—Carl Popesch, Salzburg.

Plate 29—The Reverend W. P. Walsh, Braintree.

Plate 30—A. R. Mowbray & Co. Ltd.

Plate 33—The Dean and Chapter of St. Paul's Cathedral, London.

Introduction

THE chapters which follow on this introduction will show that the history and development of the altar in Christian worship is a long and complicated process.

The wooden table of the first three centuries gives place to one of stone in the fourth century, and although wooden tables were to persist in some places even into the late middle ages, stone becomes the more usual material throughout Christendom. We shall also be able to lay to rest the controversy in the Church of England whether 'altar' or 'table' is the correct and legal term for the chief ornament of Christian worship. During the first four centuries we shall see that τράπεζα, θυσιαστήριον, mensa, ara and altare are used alike by Christian writers without any kind of doctrinal distinction.

For many centuries the altar was usually of equal dimensions, that is, it was cube-shaped; and when the liturgy was celebrated cloths were thrown over it which enveloped it on all sides. It was frequently, but not always, free-standing. As there is now the tendency to revive this kind of altar under the cult of what is loosely called the 'basilican' rite, we shall show that it does not follow that the celebrant invariably stood facing the people in the earlier centuries. The orientation of the celebrant and of the building in which Christian worship took place date from pre-Nicene times and are factors that cannot be ignored. Also, this type of altar needs to be surmounted by a ciborium, if it is not to appear mean and insignificant. This fact has been ignored in some of the examples of altars of this kind which have been erected under the liturgical movement, both in the Church of England and in the Roman Catholic Church in recent years.

Another controversy that can now be laid to rest is the question of the number of candlesticks that should stand on an Anglican altar. The argument that six is more correct and catholic than two is now an outmoded controversy. We now know that for over a thousand years nothing usually stood on the altar; and that while the Mysteries were seldom celebrated without some sort of light, this was provided by hanging lamps or from candlesticks which stood around the altar. The same must be stated in regard to an altar cross. This is a very late innovation and only since the second phase of the Oxford Movement has it come to be assumed, quite mistakenly, that *all* altars must have a cross of some kind standing on them. It cannot be too strongly emphasized that the Holy Table is not a pedestal for the support of flower vases, candlesticks and cross, all of which tend to add a note of triviality and to detract from the chief purpose of the altar.

Cut flowers in vases form no part of the appointments of the Christian altar. In ancient times they were sometimes strewn on the pavement before the altar, together with sweet smelling herbs, on festivals. A particularly hideous form of bulbous brass flower vase, which has become almost an article of faith in some of our churches, is the invention of the Victorian church furnisher. Brass is a vulgar and tawdry substitute for gold; and its use for altar ornaments should be avoided since there is nothing peculiarly sacred about this metal. Intelligent people will soon realize that flowers are best placed around the altar or in window sills, or on *low* stools and in earthenware or stone crocks. Even this use of flowers calls for restraint and supervision; and the tendency to leave flowers in a state of putrefaction near the altar calls for protest. A good deal of nonsense has been written and spoken about flowers matching the altar frontal and hangings; or that only *white* flowers are suitable for Easter. Let flowers be of blue, red and yellow as well as white; and they should be arranged gracefully and freely.

As we shall show, the idea that there is something peculiarly English and insular about an altar enshrined by riddel curtains supported between four posts or columns is now discredited; and we take this opportunity of expressing our indebtedness to *Further Thoughts on the English Altar* by the late Sir Ninian Comper. The riddel-post type of altar is a later medieval development from the ciborium, and it was found all over Northern Europe in the last part of the middle ages, and even as far south as Spain, and it was to continue in use in France as late as the eighteenth century.

The elaborations and ornate decoration of the Gothic Revival and the later phases of the Oxford Movement are now tending to be succeeded by a stark, puritanical functionalism, and many of our newer churches are lacking in colour. The omission of the altar frontal or *antependium* in one of its forms is a deplorable indication of the extreme lengths to which this kind of thing can be taken. The altar symbolizes Christ in the midst of His Church; and if His ministers are arrayed in costly vesture, why is the Table of the Lord to be treated in this manner? The Canon Law of the Church of England, the rubrics of the Roman Missal and the tradition of Eastern Orthodoxy all require the altar to be covered during the time of the divine liturgy, except during the last part of Holy Week. Where the altar is visible on both sides, it should have two 'frontals.' If the 'throw over' frontal is used it should only be employed where there is a spacious sanctuary and the altar is free-standing. Also this kind of frontal is expensive and can only be made under expert advice.

It is an odd comment on the confused state of affairs in the Church of England, that while the proposed new Canons, upon which so much time has been expended by our Convocations, insist that the Cathedral church of the diocese is to be the exemplar and pattern for the diocese in respect of liturgical practice, two prominent cathedrals, St. Paul, London, and St. Michael, Coventry, exemplify a contempt for Canon Law by having the Holy Table naked and exposed during the celebration of the Eucharist.

Stone altars should have an altar slab made from one piece of hard natural stone or marble. Concrete or synthetic materials should not be used for this purpose. Neither should a wooden table have a stone top or vice versa.

The last three decades have witnessed a growing revolt in church design and architecture against mere revivalism and the copying of the past. It is asserted that we must produce works of art for use in Christian worship which are modern and contemporary. These assertions will command widespread assent; but they can become dangerous clichés when applied to the design of the Christian altar and its surroundings. What is contemporary today can easily be outmoded tomorrow if the function of a church is not understood by our architects, as it appears not to be in more than one so-called modern design for a church. Moreover, in Christian worship and its art the element of tradition cannot be entirely eliminated or ignored, since tradition is based on the wisdom and experience of the past and not simply on conservatism. The desire to be up-to-date and contemporary in worship and in the planning of the altar and its setting can easily lead to the production of something which in striving to be different is merely grotesque and bizarre. Indeed, it can even produce something unfunctional when the fundamental traditions of the altar and its surroundings are laid aside for the sake of novelty of effect.

Finally, may we remind our readers that it is as well to remember that the temple exists for the altar and not the altar for the temple. Consequently the church should be built round the Lord's Table and planned accordingly.

PLATE I

A BASILICAN ALTAR WITHOUT A CONFESSIO

This altar with its ciborium is at Castel Sant' Elia, near Nepi in Central Italy. It is one of the oldest altars of this type still *in situ*. Built in the tenth century it is older than most of those in the great Roman basilicas which were reconstructed in the later middle ages.

The absence of the *confessio* with its opening or *fenestella* on the nave side of the altar means the celebrant stands with his back to the congregation facing the apse, as the foot-pace clearly shows.

Rods and rings for veils round all four sides of the altar are still in evidence.

PLATE 2

ALTAR WITH A CONFESSIO

This picture shows the high altar of Anagni Cathedral in Central Italy. The present canopy and altar were rebuilt in the early twelfth century. The altar is elevated so that the *confessio* with its opening beneath may be accessible.

Rods with rings for veils are still *in situ*. The Paschal candlestick stands on the right and is a permanent feature. The screens with gates will be noted before the altar.

The candlesticks and cross on the altar conflict with the celebrant celebrating *versus populum* and are a modern innovation. The church faces west.

PLATE 3

CIBORIUM WITH A REREDOS

This is the earliest example of a ciborium now in use. Originally in the destroyed
Church of Sant' Eleucadio, Classe, it is now in the left aisle of Sant' Apollinare in
Classe. The inscription at the top of the canopy informs us that a 'praesbiter' named
Peter constructed it in the time of Archbishop Valerio (d. 810). The ciborium and
the reredos may, therefore, be assigned to the opening years of the ninth century.

Under the altar is a *confessio* designed to take a reliquary.

PLATE 4

A German Super-Altar

Made in the twelfth century in North Germany from purple porphyry and framed and decorated with gilt-copper.

PLATE 5

A Precious Metal Frontal

The Church of St. Ambrose, Milan. Under this altar lies the body of St. Ambrose (d. 397). The altar has detachable embossed frontals of real gold belonging to the early ninth century; while the ends of the altar are covered with silver-gilt plates of the same period.

The four columns of blue porphyry which support the canopy were made about 386, while the canopy itself of gilded Roman stucco belongs to the twelfth century.

The cross and candlesticks belong to the baroque, and are an innovation of that period.

PLATE 6

A Spanish Tester

This tester, now in the Episcopal Museum, Vich, in Catalonia, shows that the separation of the canopy from its supports was not unknown in Southern Europe.

The underside of the tester depicts Christ in glory surrounded by the symbols of the four Evangelists.

PLATE 7

A Medieval Altar with Canopy

The high altar of Gerona Cathedral, Spain, has a fourteenth-century canopy supported on four slender columns. The canopy is of wood covered with silver-gilt. This arrangement shows the transition between the ciborium and the later riddel-post type of altar.

The reredos is of the same date, and has scenes from the Birth, Passion and Resurrection of our Lord.

For the purpose of this photograph the altar has been stripped of its usual frontal, and the riddel curtains removed at the sides so that the arrangement of the altar may be seen in relation to the canopy.

Canopies of the same type may also be seen at Palma and Majorca.

PLATE 8

THE CHAPEL OF HENRY VII, WESTMINSTER

The altar and ciborium were originally made by Pietro Torrigiano in 1526, and remained in use until destroyed by the Puritans in 1643. The present altar and its canopy follow closely on Torrigiano's original design and were erected in 1935 under the supervision of the late Sir Walter Tapper.

The canopy is surmounted by the arms of Henry VII and the symbols of the Passion of Christ, including the Cross.

PLATE 9

A RENAISSANCE ALTAR

This fresco forms one of a series in the Piccolomini Library at Siena Cathedral, painted by Pinturicchio in 1498 to illustrate the life of Aeneas Silvio Piccolomini, who later became Pope Pius II.

In this picture Aeneas Silvio is receiving a cardinal's hat. The altar is vested with the later form of frontal. At the back is a typical early Italian renaissance altar-piece. Over the altar is suspended a fabric canopy or baldaquin.

PLATE 10

AN ENGLISH BAROQUE CANOPY

Built in 1727 by Nicholas Hawksmoor, the Church of St. Mary Woolnoth in the City of London has this interesting example of an altar canopy in which the main outlines predominate over the architectural details; and thereby it differs from much continental baroque.

26

PLATE 11

11(a)

AN ENGLISH MEDIEVAL
TESTER

In the second half of the middle ages the altar canopy was frequently suspended from the sanctuary roof instead of resting directly on piers or columns.

Our picture shows the fifteenth-century example still *in situ* over the altar at Clun, Salop, made of oak and divided into thirty decorated panels. It will be noted that the tester is four-square.

11(b)

THE CANOPY IN NORWAY

This picture shows the interior of the stave-church at Hopperstad, built about 1130. All three altars are cube-shaped, while that on the north side of the nave has preserved its ciborium.

PLATE 12

OLD ST. PETER'S, ROME

This fresco forms one of a series in the Stanze of the Vatican made by Raphael and his pupils between 1508 and 1524. While the scene depicted, the Donation of Constantine, is unhistorical, the detailed accuracy of the interior of Old St. Peter's is not in doubt since it accords with evidence from other sources; and also the picture was made before the sanctuary and altar of the old basilica were demolished.

The vested altar stands under its ciborium on the chord of the Western apse. It is raised over the *confessio*, the grill of which can be seen under the altar. The altar screen with its twisted column has votive lamps hanging under the architrave. The Pope is vested in the pontificals of the late fifteenth century; and suspended over his throne is a fabric canopy or baldaquin.

28

PLATE 13

13(a)

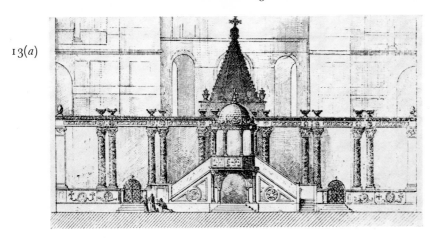

THE SCREEN IN THE EAST

This reconstruction of the screen in the Church of the Holy Wisdom (Hagia Sophia) at Constantinople, built by the Emperor Justinian the Great in A.D. 537, was made by Rohault de Fleury in *La Messe*, Tome III. It is based on the description of the screen given by Paul the Silentary in the sixth century and that of Constantine Porphyrogenitus in the tenth century. It shows that the solid 'picture screen' or *iconostasis* was not then part of the liturgical arrangement of the most famous church in Eastern Christendom.

13(b)

AN EARLY BYZANTINE SCREEN

Belonging to the fifth century, this screen and altar show that the difference in the screening of the altar in Eastern and Western Christendom was a much later development (see page 82).

The cube-shaped altar has a concave top. While the bishop's throne is behind the altar, at the time of the liturgy he took the eastward position since churches in the Byzantine rite have always been orientated.

PLATE 14

TRIPTYCH AND RELIQUARY

    Made of Champlevé enamel and gilt-copper. This early thirteenth-century portable triptych belongs to the School of the Meuse.

    At the top is Christ in majesty. In the centre is a glazed receptacle for a relic of the True Cross. Angels at the sides hold instruments of the Passion. Below is the Crucifixion scene surrounded by the symbols of the four Evangelists. At the bottom, the holy women visit the tomb.

    On the wings of the triptych are the figures of the twelve Apostles.

PLATE 15

A Chasse or Portable Reliquary

Made of copper-gilt with Champlevé enamel motifs in the thirteenth century. This type of reliquary sometimes stood on the altar, or on the retable over and behind the altar. It contained parts of a saint's body, or items of his clothing, or a relic of the True Cross.

PLATE 16

THE MASS OF ST. GILES

This celebrated Flemish painting by the Master of St. Giles was made in 1500. It shows with detailed accuracy the moment of the elevation of the Host. The absence of cross and candlesticks on the altar will be noted. The altar has riddel curtains supported on rods and posts.

Over and behind the altar rises the canopy, which no longer covers the altar as in the primitive period, but the shrine or reliquary of the patron saint. The reredos separates altar and shrine.

1

The Lord's Table

Name, Shape and Materials

The starting point for any consideration of the Christian Altar is the Holy Eucharist in the Upper Room on the first Maundy Thursday. Here a meal took place with a sacrificial background at a wooden table. Wooden tables were doubtless used at the celebrations of the Eucharist in private houses during the first three centuries of the Christian era. St. Paul, referring to certain disorders at Corinth connected with the Eucharist, speaks of the Lord's Table, τράπεζα κυρίου (1 *Cor.* x. 21). But this is an oblique reference to the Sacrament rather than the structure of the table. The writer of the Epistle to the Hebrews says, 'We have an altar, whereof they have no right to eat who serve the tabernacle' (*Heb.* xiii. 10). The writer of the Apocalypse states 'I saw under the altar the souls of them that had been slain for the word of God' (*Rev.* vi. 9). In both these passages the term for 'altar' in the Greek text is θυσιαστήριον.

The precise meaning of the passage in Hebrews xiii. 10 has been the subject of much dispute. Some commentators hold that the passage refers to the Eucharist and its altar.[1] A large number of writers following on the late Dr. B. F. Westcott have argued that the 'altar' in this passage means the Cross. But more recently this view has been increasingly challenged.[2] It has now been pointed out that the difficulty of accepting this passage as a reference to the Eucharist turns upon the overwhelming strength of the habit of interpreting the Cross as the ultimate Christian Altar. Such an interpretation is a medieval idea. It may not be inappropriate to draw attention to the section of the Lambeth Conference Report of 1958 dealing with the Holy Communion in which it is stated: 'The sacrifice of Christ as the offering of willing obedience included not only His death on the Cross, but all that contributed to it, of which it is the culmination. The finished work of Calvary is consummated in the resurrection and ascension.' Like-wise, it is most relevant to consider the late Charles Gore's statement in regard to Hebrews xiii. 10: ' "We have an altar, whereof they have no right to eat which serve the tabernacle," but we, it is implied, have—it cannot reasonably be disputed that he is referring to the

---

[1] H. L. Pass in *Encyclopaedia of Religion and Ethics* (1908), Vol. I, p. 338.
[2] S. C. Gayford, *Sacrifice and Priesthood* (1924), pp. 165–6; also F. C. N. Hicks, *The Fullness of Sacrifice*, p. 235; also E. L. Mascall, *Corpus Christi* (1953), pp. 82–5.

familiar but solemn rite of the Holy Communion in which Christians ate of the body and blood of their atoning sacrifice. The "altar" must mean the place where the atonement is made, and this, according to this writer, is rather in the heavenly place than on the Cross. According to the local imagery which he employs, it is something in heaven corresponding to the "golden altar" which belonged to the Jewish holy of holies. But in a secondary sense it must mean the actual "table of the Lord" at which Christians were fed with the sacrificial food, and which gained all its significance from being the earthly image of the reality in the heaven.'[1]

Other commentators, doubtless because of the tendency to equate sacrifice solely with death or immolation, have been unable to offer any explanation of the meaning of θυσιαστήριον in Hebrews xiii. 10.[2]

Outside the New Testament one of the earliest writers on Church Order is St. Ignatius of Antioch (d. c. A.D. 110). He employs the term θυσιαστήριον several times in connexion with Christian worship. Thus in the seventh chapter of his Epistle to the Magnesians he says: 'Hasten all to come together as to one temple of God, as to one altar, to one Jesus Christ.'[3] It has sometimes been suggested that the term 'altar' means the building or sanctuary in the Ignatian Epistles. But in the passage we have quoted Ignatius draws a distinction between 'temple' (ναός) and 'altar' (θυσιαστήριον).

Further, it has been stated that the 'altar' to which Ignatius refers is a 'spiritual' one having no direct reference to the Eucharist. This view has been prominently associated with the late Dr. Lightfoot in his celebrated work on the Apostolic Fathers.[4] But critics[5] during the present century have been at pains to point out that Lightfoot's interpretation of the Ignatian Epistles and other early Christian writings, particularly those passages which have reference to Christian worship, are conditioned by the strong presuppositions which he held in regard to the Christian Ministry; and that consequently his interpretation of the Apostolic Fathers in regard to Christian worship lacks that objectivity which he displayed in other aspects of his great studies.

More recent commentators[6] have accepted the view that Ignatius is referring to the Eucharist and its altar when he says in the fourth

[1] C. Gore: *The Body of Christ* (1901), pp. 260–1.
[2] *Peake's Commentary on the Bible* (new ed. 1962), p. 1018.
[3] K. Lake: *The Apostolic Fathers* (1959), vol. I, pp. 202–3.
[4] J. B. Lightfoot: *The Apostolic Fathers* (1886–90), 5 vols.
[5] R. C. Moberly: *Ministerial Priesthood* (2nd ed. 1919), pp. xxxiii–ix, 43–50, 276–82.
[6] H. L. Pass, op. cit., p. 338; also Jungmann: *The Mass of the Roman Rite*, vol. I, p. 25; also C. Gore: op. cit., pp. 58–9, pp. 292–3.

chapter of his Epistle to the Philadelphians: 'Be careful to use one
Eucharist, for there is one flesh of our Lord Jesus Christ, and one cup
for union with His blood, one altar, as there is one bishop with the
presbytery and deacons.'[1] Another passage in which Ignatius associates
θυσιαστήριον with the Eucharist is in the fifth chapter of his Epistle
to the Ephesians: 'Unless a man be within the precinct of the altar
he lacks the bread of God.'[2]

It is important to take note of the derivation and antecedent use
of θυσιαστήριον prior to its appearance in the writings of the New
Testament and the Apostolic Fathers. This is to be found in the Septuagint text of the Old Testament.[3] The matter is of interest particularly
in view of the fact that the writer of the Epistle to the Hebrews knew
the LXX and quotes from it as did the Apostolic Fathers. θυσιαστήριον
in the LXX is associated with Jewish and pagan altars of sacrifice.
The term appears to be unknown in classical Greek. Typical examples
in the LXX are: τὴν βάσιν τοῦ θυσιαστήριον, Ex. xxix. 12; ἐπὶ τοῦ θυσιαστη-
ρίου, Lev. vi 9; τὸ θυσιαστήριον τοῦ βάαλ, Judges vi. 25; καὶ ἀνέστησε
θυσιαστήριον τῇ βάαλ, II (IV) Kings xxi. 3.

If the dating of the *Didache* between A.D. 60 and 100 by recent
authorities is correct,[4] then, the comparison which the writer makes in
his fourteenth chapter between the Sunday Eucharist and 'a pure
sacrifice' in Malachi i. 11 also has an appropriate significance: 'On
the Lord's Day of the Lord come together, break bread and hold
Eucharist, after confessing your transgressions that your offering may
be pure. . . . For this is that which was spoken by the Lord, "In every
place and time offer me a pure sacrifice (θυσία) for I am a great king,
saith the Lord." '[5] It will be observed that in the LXX θυσία is the
normal term used to describe Jewish and pagan sacrifices.[6] The
Fathers do not scruple to use the terms θυσιαστήριον, ara, altare, and
even sometimes βωμός for the unbloody sacrifice of the Eucharist.
Synesius of Cyrene (d. 414) uses the expression βωμὸς ὁ ἀναίμακτος, the
unbloody altar.[7]

The Latin Fathers use the terms *ara* and *altare* for the Eucharist
and its altar without diffidence. Thus Tertullian (d. *c.* 220) says,

[1] K. Lake: op. cit., pp. 242–3.
[2] D. Stone: *A History of the Doctrine of the Holy Eucharist*, Vol. I, p. 46.
[3] See G. A. Abbott-Smith: *Manual Greek Lexicon of the New Testament* (3rd ed. 1957), p. 211; also
W. F. Arndt and F. W. Gingrich: *A Greek-English Lexicon of the New Testament and other Early Christian
Literature* (1957), pp. xvi-xvii and p. 367.
[4] F. L. Cross: *The Early Christian Fathers* (1960), pp. 8–11.
[5] K. Lake: ibid., pp. 242–3.
[6] Abbott-Smith: op. cit., pp. 210–11; also Arndt and Gingrich, op. cit., pp. 366–7.
[7] Syn. *Catastasis* (P.G., Tome 66, 1573).

'Does then the Eucharist cancel a service devoted to God, or bind it more to God? Will not your Station be more solemn if you have withal stood at God's altar (*ara Dei*)?'[1] But the more usual term for the Christian altar in the early Latin commentators is *altare* and this is the case in the Vulgate, where *ara* is used only for heathen altars, e.g. Judges vi. 25, Acts xvii. 23. St. Cyprian of Carthage (d. 258) writes of the lapsed Bishop Fortunatianus that without repentance he comes 'from the altars of the devil to approach the altar of God.'[2] Here Cyprian contrasts the *arae diaboli* with the *altare Dei*.

In some of the Greek Fathers, such as St. Gregory of Nazianzus (d. *c.* 390) and St. John Chrysostom (d. 407), the term τράπεζα is used, coupled with such adjectives as 'mystical,' 'tremendous' and 'priestly.'[3] Having in mind the statement that is sometimes made that the Apostolic Fathers only used the term θυσιαστήριον in a metaphorical sense, and that the later Greek Fathers did not use the term to describe the material altar in a church building, we draw attention to the description of the Church at Tyre which Eusebius of Caesarea (d. 339) gives in his *Ecclesiastical History* (see also page 64) in which he refers to the altar as τὸ τῶν ἁγίων θυσιαστήριον. Another writer of the same period, Synesius of Cyrene, in his treatise *Catastasis*, also uses the term to describe the altar.[4]

The early writers were, however, careful to draw a distinction between the Eucharist on the one hand, and the bloody sacrifices of the Old Covenant and the idol sacrifices of paganism on the other, as we can see in the writings of Origen (d. 253),[5] Lactantius and Minucius Felix.

It is of interest to note that St. Augustine (d. 430) uses the term *altare* in connexion with a wooden table, for he tells of an outrage by the Donatists against a catholic bishop: 'As he stood at the altar they beat him cruelly with clubs and such like weapons, and at last with broken pieces of timber from the altar itself.'[6] In other places, however, he uses the term *mensa Domini*, the Lord's Table.[7]

The wooden tables depicted in the frescoes of the catacombs are of various shapes: some square, some round, and some semi-circular.

---

[1] Tertul., *de Orat*, c. 19 (P.L., Tome 1, 1181).
[2] Cyprian: Ep. 66. 1 (P.L., Tome 4, 389); also C.S.E.L. III, p. 722.
[3] P.G., Tome 37, 1161 and Tome 49, 322; also Tome 58, 739.
[4] Ibid., Tome 66, 1572.
[5] Origen, Contra Cels., lib. 8. 17 (P.G., Tome 11, 1540).
[6] Ep. 185, Ad Bon. (P.L., Tome 33, 803) Stantem ad altare, fustibus et hujus modi telis, lignis denique ejusdem altaris effractis, immaniter ceciderunt.
[7] P.L., Tome 38, Cols. 145 and 193.

Some have three legs, but four legs are more common.[1] An early wooden altar is preserved in St. John Lateran, Rome, and there is part of another in the same city at Santa Pudentiana.

Although stone came to be accepted as the more usual material from the fourth century, wooden altars seem never to have disappeared entirely in medieval England. St. Wulfstan, Bishop of Worcester (1062–95), felt obliged to campaign in his diocese against the use of wooden altars which it was alleged had been the custom in England from time immemorial: *Erant tunc temporis altaria lignea; iam inde a priscis diebus in Anglia.*[2] Wooden altars were also in use as late as the fifteenth century, as was the case at St. John's Hungate, York,[3] and at Aldwark in 1432, and another at St. Christopher-le-Stocks, London, in 1483.[4]

The earliest decree requiring stone altars is one alleged to have been made by Pope Sylvester (314–335), to which there is a reference in the Roman Breviary, Dedication of the Lateran, November 9, nocturn 2, lesson 6: 'The Blessed Sylvester afterwards decreed, when he was consecrating the altar of the Prince of the Apostles, that altars were thence-forward to be made of stone only, but notwithstanding this the Lateran Cathedral hath the altar made of wood.' But doubt has been cast on the authenticity of this decree,[5] which is most probably a forgery.

An early reference to stone altars is found in St. Gregory of Nyssa (d. 394), he says: 'This altar whereat we stand is by nature only common stone, nothing different from other stones, whereof our walls are made and our pavements adorned; but after it is consecrated and dedicated to the service of God, it becomes a holy table, an immaculate altar.'[6]

Wooden altars continue in use in the Ethiopian Church at the present time.[7]

Association with the Saints

There can be little doubt, however, that the custom of having stone altars is directly connected with the celebration of the Eucharist on or at the tomb of a martyr in the catacombs,[8] thus linking altar

---

[1] D.A.C.L., Tome 1, 3158–61.
[2] 'Vita S. Wulstani,' in *De gestis Pontific. Angl.* (R.H.S., Vol. 40, p. 54 (1928) ed. R. R. Darlington).
[3] Braun: op. cit., Vol. 1, p. 212: see also D.A.C.L., Tome I, 3060–1.
[4] F. E. Howard and F. H. Crossley: *English Church Woodwork* (2nd ed., 1927), p. 135.
[5] Bona: *Rerum liturgicarum*, liber, cap. xx, p. 149 (Rome, 1671); also D.A.C.L., Tome I, 3168.
[6] *In baptism. Christi* (P.G., Tome 46, 581).
[7] A. A. King: *Rites of Eastern Christendom*, vol. 1, pp. 553–4.   [8] D.A.C.L., Tome 1, 3161–3.

with tomb. With the building of important churches in the fourth century at Rome and elsewhere, the idea was carried a step further and the altar came to be built over the confessor's or martyr's burial place. Hence the expression *confessio* or *martyrium* to indicate the sacred place over which the altar stood. In some cases the coffin or reliquary was above the level of the floor of the church and the altar was elevated so that there could be an opening, usually on the nave side, known as the *fenestella*. (See Plates 2 and 12.) Through this opening it was customary for people to insert cloths and other objects, which, being brought into contact with the saint's tomb or coffin, were believed to acquire a healing value. In other cases the tomb was below the floor of the church, which meant there was a staircase by the altar. This arrangement of the *confessio* with its opening below the altar, was one of the contributory causes for the celebrant having to stand on the other side of the altar facing the people, as there could be no foot-pace on the nave-side of the altar.[1]

It is necessary to take note, however, that recent researches and explorations at St. Peter's, Rome, have shown fairly conclusively that the reputed shrine or *martyrium* of St. Peter stood apart from the altar in early times and that it was completely above the level of the floor of the church. Only in the sixth century, possibly in the time of Pope Pelagius II (579–590), did the altar become directly associated with the shrine,[2] when the floor of the sanctuary was raised up so that part of the *martyrium* was sunk below floor-level; and the altar thus became associated with the shrine by being built up over the *confessio*.[3] The siting of the altar in relation to the martyrdom before this sixth century innovation is uncertain.

In the earlier centuries stone altars varied to some degree in their shape, and examples of circular and semi-circular altar tables are still extant, as at Besançon Cathedral.[4] The altar slab was sometimes supported on a single large pier or column, while in other cases there were four smaller supports, thus resembling the legs of a table; in other cases there were blocks of masonry upon which the altar top rested. The form of the altar in the older Roman basilicas was, however, more like a chest or box, in which all four sides under the altar slab, or mensa, were filled in with panels of marble, usually undecorated. (See Plate 1.)

---

[1] Braun: op. cit., Vol. 1, p. 412 ff.   [2] D.A.C.L., Tome 15, 3332.
[3] J. B. Ward Perkins in *The Journal of Roman Studies*, vol. 42 (1952), pp. 21–4.
[4] Braun: op. cit., Vol. 1, p. 245–6.

The altar was for many centuries usually of equal dimensions, and therefore cube-shaped or four square. In Eastern Christendom this custom is still continued, and while the mensa must be made of stone, other materials may be used for the base of the altar.[1]

Examples of pagan altars being rededicated for Christian use are not unknown; and three such examples are to be seen in the Lateran Museum, Rome.[2]

The presence of the bodies of martyrs at Rome, and elsewhere, such as Carthage in North Africa, led at a comparatively early date to the demand that altars should be dedicated with the relics of the saints, either by building the altar over the *confessio*, or by inserting in some part of the structure of the altar relics of the saints, such as the *brandea* or cloths, which had rested on the tomb of the saint. At a later date the dismemberment of the bodies of saints meant that such relics were parts of the body or bones of the saint. But in the fourth century there was an aversion to this practice.

When the relics of saints in the form of portions of the body came into fashion the relic was sometimes enclosed in a cavity with an opening immediately under the mensa, thus forming a *confessio* on a smaller scale. (See Plate 3.)

In the early fourth century churches were divided into two kinds, (*a*) those where a celebrated saint was buried under the altar, (*b*) ordinary churches which were simply places of assembly for liturgical worship. By a kind of ritualistic fiction the second class of church became the tomb of a saint by the increasing custom of burying in the altar cloths or other relics that had been in contact with the sarcophagus of the saint. To possess an object of this kind was thought to be like possessing the body of the saint. By the seventh-eighth century the dismemberment of the bodies of saints led to the custom of inserting such relics in the top of the altar-slab in a cavity or opening known as the *sepulcrum* or sepulchre.[3] In this were entombed the bones of saints, together with three grains of incense representing the spices connected with the rites of burial, and three fragments of a consecrated host.[4]

In A.D. 386, St. Ambrose completed at Milan a basilica, which occupied the same site as the present Church of Sant' Ambrogio. He proposed to dedicate this basilica in the simple manner of earlier times

---

[1] S. Salaville: *Introduction to the Eastern Liturgies*, pp. 133-4.
[2] Bond: op. cit., p. 6; also D.A.C.L., Tome 3, 1682-92.
[3] Braun: op. cit., Vol. 1, pp. 656 ff.
[4] M. Andrieu: *Les Ordines Romani*, Vol. 4, pp. 389 and 400 (Louvain, 1956).

by the celebration of the Eucharist with a sermon and special prayers. This did not please the people, who remonstrated with him, saying, 'Consecrate this as you did the Roman basilica.' The so-called 'Roman' basilica was the Church of the Apostles at Milan, now known as San Nazaro Grande, which had been dedicated with the relics of St. Peter and St. Paul.[1] The people clearly wished that the new church should be dedicated, after the manner which was then coming into fashion, by the deposition of relics in or under the altar.

The apparent shortage of relics in Britain led, however, to the Council of Chelsea in July 816 declaring that, if other suitable relics were not available, the Sacrament of the Eucharist was sufficient.[2] In 1433, Lyndwood, the celebrated English Canonist, recognized this absence of relics in the consecration of an altar and adds that the placing of the Eucharist in the sepulchre is sufficient: *Ubi tamen non habentes reliquas, solent aliqui apponere Corpus Christi.*[3] In another place he quotes the decree of Stephen Langton, Archbishop of Canterbury (1207–1228), that where no relics are to be had worn-out 'corporal' cloths may be encased in the altar;[4] and he adds that relics *non sunt de substantia consecrationis altaris.*

The Pontifical which belonged to Christopher Bainbridge, Archbishop of York (1508–14), contains an interesting and significant rubric in the rite for the consecration of a church. This rubric occurs immediately before the bishop consecrates the altar; and it shows that at this late date the matter of relics being entombed in the altar is not regarded as essential to the consecration of an altar: *Sequitur oratio dicenda sive reliquiae fuerint sive non.*[5]

Other examples of late English medieval pontificals are available in which the absence of relics in an altar are to be noted. Thus in two fifteenth-century pontificals written for Bishops of London the scarcity of old relics and the infrequent canonization of new saints meant that altars were often consecrated without the deposition of relics.[6] Nor was the absence of relics in altars peculiar to England since

---

[1] F. H. Dudden: *The Life and Times of St. Ambrose*, Vol. 1, pp. 298–9 (1935).

[2] A. W. Haddan and W. Stubbs: *Councils and Ecclesiastical Documents relating to Gt. Britain*, Vol. 3, p. 580 (Oxford, 1870).

[3] *Provinciale*, III, 26, note m. (Oxoniae, 1679, p. 249).

[4] Ibid., note a., p. 249. Vetera quoque corporalia, quae non fuerint idonea, in altaribus, quando consecrantur, loco reliquiarum reponantur.

[5] *Liber Pontificalis Chr. Bainbridge* (Surtees Society, Vol. 61, p. 74. (1875).

[6] Corpus Christi Coll. Cambridge MS. No. 79, f. 46, also Brit. Mus., Lansdowne 451, f. 136. Sciendum est tamen quod uariis modis recluduntur reliquie infra altare, licet istis temporibus hoc raro fiat propter reliquiarum antiquarum paucitatem et nouorum sanctorum raram canonizationem tamen si debeat fieri potest expleri prout supra notatur in magna rubrica in principio dedicacionis more romano mensa altaris pendendo eleuata et postea deposita et cementata.

a pontifical which belonged to the German diocese of Trier in the fifteenth century says that the Host may be placed in altars where relics are lacking;[1] while an Italian pontifical of the same century indicates that relics may be dispensed with in the consecration of churches.[2] In a series of Roman Missals printed in France between 1507 and 1546 we find an allusion to the possibility of the absence of relics in the altar. For at the beginning of the Mass *Ordo* the celebrant is instructed to say alternative prayers depending on the presence or absence of relics in the altar.[3]

Later Modifications

The fourteenth-century altar in the Lady Chapel of Ely Cathedral measured sixteen feet, four and a half inches, that at Tewkesbury Abbey thirteen feet, eight inches, and that in the FitzAlan Chapel, Arundel, twelve feet, six inches. These are typical examples of the altar that came into use from the fourteenth century onwards. Needless to state, the altar slab was always in one piece. Pope Innocent III writing at the end of the twelfth century insisted that the unbroken wholeness was a symbol of the unity of the Church, which must not be divided by error or schism.[4]

No doubt another factor which contributed to the lengthening of the altar in the later middle ages was the screens and reredoses which, in the greater churches, usually stretched between the north and south wall of the sanctuary behind the altar. Significance could only be given to the altar beneath by lengthening it in proportion to the width of the sanctuary; whereas in the earlier centuries the four-square altar gained significance, and attention was focused on it, by the ciborium standing on its columns.

The requirement that the altar should be furnished with a row of six candlesticks (seven when a bishop sings High Mass) and a standing cross only became *de rigueur* in the seventeenth century in the Roman rite.[5] Also, only since 1746 has the altar cross in that rite been required to be a crucifix, that is, a cross with a *corpus* or figure on it.[6]

[1] Brit. Mus., Add. MS. 16610, f. 97.
[2] Vatican 10511 (olim Borgia II) f. 9. Si vero ecclesia consecranda non sint reliquiae, omnibus perfectis ante foras ecclesiae consecranda et etiam aqua simplici ut supradictum est.
[3] J. W. Legg: *Tracts on the Mass* (1904), p. 181. For further examples of the absence of relics in altars, see J. W. Legg: *Three Chapters in Recent Liturgical Research*, (1903), pp. 60–6.
[4] *De Sacro Altaris Mysterio*, ii, 3 (P.L., Tome 247, 803). Per altare signatur Ecclesia, juxta quod Dominus dixit in Exodo, 'Si altare lapideum feceris mihi, non aedificabis illud de sectis lapidibus' (*Exod.* xx. 25). Quod sectionem lapidum prohibet in altari divisionem fidelium reprobat, ne ecclesia dividatur per errores et schismata.
[5] D. R. Dendy: *The Use of Lights in Christian Worship*, pp. 62–3.
[6] Cf. Pocknee: op. cit., pp. 36–7.

Vases of flowers placed on the altar, or immediately behind on a shelf, were unknown in the primitive era or in the middle ages. In the Roman rite recognition of the custom belongs to the Counter-Reformation. The seventeenth-century *Caerimoniale* (liber I, cap. 12) says: 'Vases, too, carefully decorated with blossoms and leaves of sweet fragrance or artificially made of silk may be added.'[1] Artificial flowers were condemned, however, in June 1932 by the Cardinal Vicar of Rome. No cut flowers are seen on the altars of the greater Roman basilicas. Instead, sprigs of bay are thrown on the pavement at festivals, in the same manner as sweet-smelling leaves were thrown on the stone floors of churches in England and other parts of Europe in the middle ages.

In the Church of England cut flowers were not placed on the altar in the seventeenth and eighteenth centuries, although churches were decorated with evergreens, bay and holly at Christmas and other occasions. The introduction of flower vases on to Anglican altars took place in the nineteenth century.

Since the Reformation the terms 'altar' and 'table' have been the subject of controversy in England. This has been due to an inadequate conception of the Eucharist, and a misconception as to the nature of sacrifice. The Lambeth Conference Report, 1958, rightly says: 'The time has come to claim that controversies about the Eucharistic sacrifice can be laid aside.' The Christian altar is both banquet and sacrifice. The Holy Communion is the Sacrament of Sacrifice. The persistence of both terms, *mensa* and *altare* in the Roman rite, and of the terms τράπεζα and θυσιαστήριον in the Greek-speaking East, shows that this fact has not been forgotten in historic Christendom.

In the seventeenth and eighteenth centuries most parish churches in England had wooden altars; but stone and marble altars were certainly erected in a number of churches in the City of London and elsewhere during the post-Reformation era. Thus at All Hallows-the-Great in 1708: 'The Communion-Table is a marble slab, supported by a Figure in stone of the Angel Gabriel, and its foot pace is also of marble.'[2]

Consecration of Altars

As early as the year 500 there is evidence that it was customary in some places[3] for the bishop to anoint the altar top with chrism

---

[1] *Caerimoniale Episcoporum* (Rome, 1606), p. 73.
[2] For further examples see *Hierurgia Anglicana*, ed. V. Staley, Vol. 1, pp. 30–4 (1902); also J. W. Legg, *English Church Life*, pp. 134–6 (1914).
[3] Cf. Andrieu, *Les Ordines Romani*, pp. 324–5, Vol. 4 (1956).

during the rite of consecration. This followed on the lustration of the mensa with holy water. Thus the consecration of the altar was approximated to that of the rite of baptism-confirmation. The altar was anointed in the middle and at the four corners with the sign of the Cross. The Council of Epaone in 517 in its twenty-sixth Canon forbade this anointing unless the altar was made of stone.[1] But this ceremony was of Gallican origin, and it was not adopted at Rome until the eighth or ninth century.[2]

At first the bishop probably made the sign of the Cross in five places on the mensa without any incision or mark on the stone. But at a later date it became the custom to cut consecration crosses with a chisel prior to the ceremony; and these were anointed during the rite of consecration. But this could only have taken place when the surface of the altar top was level, since many of the earlier stone altars had a low ledge round the four sides, the inside surface being concave. (See Plate 13(b).)

As the altar came to be lengthened in the second part of the middle ages, there was the tendency to multiply the number of consecration crosses and anointings, seven and even nine such crosses being known in some instances, as at Broughton Castle.[3] The present Roman rite requires five crosses.

While the Council of Epaone in 517 and succeeding Councils were to insist that only altars of stone could be consecrated, there were occasions and places in which it was necessary to celebrate the Eucharist on a wooden table. Such occasions arose in the case of missionaries on journeys in countries where no churches had been built, armies moving on campaigns, such as the Crusaders, and on board ship. There were, too, oratories in the houses and castles of important people where Mass had sometimes to be celebrated. To meet this situation there was invented a 'super-altar,' that is, a small rectangle or square of stone, which having been previously consecrated by a bishop could be carried about by a priest. It could be inserted in the *sepulcrum* of an unconsecrated table or altar, or it could simply be placed in the middle of the table so that the chalice and paten stood upon it during the Eucharistic action.[4]

These super-altars were often made of a semi-precious stone such as porphyry or jasper. This last stone was much favoured because

[1] Mansi, Tome 8, 562. Altaria nisi lapidea crismatis unctione non sacrentur.
[2] Andrieu: op. cit., pp. 385 and 400.
[3] Rock: *Church of our Fathers*, Vol. 1, p. 192.
[4] Braun: op. cit., Vol. 1, pp. 444–517.

of the reference to it in Revelation xx. 19, in connexion with the heavenly Jerusalem.[1] The stone was frequently encased in plates of silver or copper-gilt. (See Plate 4.) Such super-altars were much sought after when they had been used by some famous and holy person, and were sometimes kept in a cathedral treasury. In other instances the portable altar was buried with the saint.

Eminent people who had an oratory were sometimes allowed to possess their own super-altar; but this required special papal and episcopal authority.[2]

It is necessary to notice the type of super-altar that was in use in Anglo-Saxon England since its use of *wood* conflicts with the necessity of having a consecrated stone. The Anglo-Saxon portable altar was made of oak, usually about six inches square, having incised upon it signs of the Cross and the name of the saint in whose honour it was blessed. It was usually encased in plates of silver, which were marked with crosses and an inscription. Simeon of Durham (d. *c.* 1138) in his history of the Acts of the Kings of England describes such a super-altar in connexion with the translation of the relics of St. Acca.[3]

Important corroboration of these facts about the wooden portable altar of the Anglo-Saxons is to be seen in the Chapter Library at Durham, where the most famous of these objects is now housed, the one which belonged to St. Cuthbert (d. 687). It was buried with the saint; and has recently been examined by the experts of the British Museum. It is of oak bound with silver plates.[4]

Another kind of portable altar, often bound in gold plates and decorated with precious stones, stood on four small feet or supports. This was placed on the altars of cathedrals and great churches on important occasions, and in honour of bishops when they celebrated the liturgy. One such altar of gold was kept in an iron chest at Salisbury in the thirteenth century,[5] as the treasurer, Abraham, testifies in his inventory.

In the East portable altars of wood incised with crosses and other symbols have been in use for many centuries amongst the Syrians, Copts and Armenians. But in modern times it has become customary

---

[1] Rock: op. cit., Vol. 1, pp. 201–2.
[2] Cf. *Liber Pont. Chr. Bainbridge*, Vol. 61, Surtees Soc., pp. 386–7.
[3] *Hist. de Gestis Reg. Anglorum* (Rolls Society, Vol. 75, ii, 2, 23).
[4] C. F. Battiscombe: *The Relics of St. Cuthbert*, pp. 326–35 (1956).
[5] C. Wordsworth: *Salisbury Processions and Ceremonies*, p. 177 (1901), Item archa una longa similiter ferrea in qua antiquitus superaltare aureum reponebatur.

to place such wooden super-altars on the consecrated altar of a church.[1]
In the Eastern Orthodox or Byzantine rite portable stone altars are
not used. Instead, a square of linen or silk, known as the *antimension*,
folded in two, in which are sewn up relics anointed with chrism, was
originally intended to convert into an altar an ordinary table on which
it might be placed. In the present Eastern Orthodox rite, however,
the *antimension* tends to be used on consecrated altars.[2]

The Vesting and Clothing of the Altar

Custom, wellnigh universal in Christendom, has always clothed
the Holy Table with some kind of covering; at least, during the celebration of the Holy Mysteries. It was fitting that the altar should receive
every mark of respect; and even in the pre-Constantinian era people
were conscious of this, as Origen (d. 254) testifies.[3] Consequently
the Lord's Table had precious cloths spread over it. St. John
Chrysostom had to give a warning that over-zealousness in this matter
sometimes led to other things being left undone.[4]

In the earlier centuries, when the altar was usually free-standing,
it was enveloped on all four sides. Such cloths, usually termed *pallae*,
were sometimes made of silk and decorated with symbolic devices.
Two such examples are to be seen depicted in the mosaics of the sixth
century at San Vitale, Ravenna, and Sant' Apollinare in Classe,
Ravenna.[5] Optatus (*circa* 368) points out to the Donatists that their
altars could not be polluted by catholics touching them, for everyone
knew that, since the wood of the altar was covered during the liturgy,
only the covering could be touched.[6]

It seems evident that even in the primitive period not only was
the altar covered with a linen cloth or pall for the celebration of the
Eucharist; but also the Lord's Table was vested with silk cloths.
Theodoret in his Church History[7] tells us that amongst the gifts made
by Constantine the Great when the Church of the Holy Sepulchre was
built at Jerusalem (*circa* A.D. 325) there was a royal pall (βασιλικὸν

---

[1] Braun: op. cit., Vol. i, pp. 517–9; also H. W. Codrington: *Studies of the Syrian Liturgies* (1952), pp. 4–5.
[2] Braun: Vol. i, pp. 519–22; also Salaville: op. cit., pp. 152–3.
[3] Origen: *In Jesu Nave*, 10.3 (P.G., Tome 12, 881).
[4] Chrysostom: *In Matt. hom.* 50, 4 (P.G., Tome 58, 509).
[5] G. Bovini: *The Churches of Ravenna*, pp. 126–7, 160 (Novara, Italy, 1960).
[6] Optatus, lib. 6 (P.L. Tome, 11, 1067–8. Quis fidelium nescit in peragendis mysteriis ipsa ligna linteamine cooperiri? Inter ipsa sacramenta velamen poluit tangi, non lignum.
[7] Theodoret: *Eccl. Hist.* lib. i, c. 29 (P.G., Tome 82, 987).

παραπέτασμα) for the altar. Palladius writing about 421 mentions some Roman ladies, who renouncing the world, bequeathed their silks to make coverings for the altar.[1]

The *Liber Pontificalis* testifies that during the eighth and ninth centuries coverings for the altar made of gold thread and decorated with jewels and pearls and embroidered with figures of our Lord, the B.V. Mary and the Apostles were given to the great Roman basilicas by succeeding Popes.[2]

While the altar remained cubical in form the 'throw-over' type of pall continued in use; and until at least the ninth century it was customary to spread the linen cloth only during the liturgy, and not to leave it on the altar as is the modern custom. This linen cloth, known as the *Palla corporalis*, was thrown over the altar, much as an ordinary table-cloth is spread today, by the deacons,[3] and it fell down all round the sides of the table. But in the Gothic period, when the altar tended to be lengthened, two things happened: (*a*) the linen pall became divided into two parts, one part being a long strip which covered the top of the altar and fell down over each end of the mensa, while the other part became the 'corporal' which covered the elements; (*b*) the silk pall becomes the *antependium* or frontal covering the front elevation of the altar only when it stood close to a wall or screen. But it should be noted that where the longer type of altar was free-standing a 'frontal' was provided for both back and front. This fact has sometimes been ignored in modern restorations of nave altars in some of our cathedrals.

Where the altar stood close to a wall, while there was only one frontal, there was sometimes a 'super-frontal' which hung above the altar in place of a sculptured reredos, as we can see in the medieval examples still remaining at Chipping Campden, Gloucestershire.

Frontals of precious metal were also used. The most famous example now extant is at Sant' Ambrogio, Milan, where gold embossed plates of the ninth century cover both the main elevations of the altar, while there are silver-gilt plates for the two end elevations, since this altar with its ciborium is free-standing under the triumphal arch. (See Plate 5.) Braun gives a number of pictures of other precious

---

[1] Palladius: *Hist. Lausiac.* c. 119 (P.G., Tome 34, 1228).

[2] Duchesne: *Le Liber Pontificalis*, Tome 2, 10. Super altare beati Petri fecit vestem cum vite ex auro purissimo cum gemmis pretiosissimis et margaritis, habentem in medio vultum salvatoris et S. genitricis Dei Mariae seu xii apostolorum, ubi et misit aurum lib. xxv; also ibid., Tome 1, 432, 435, 500; Tome 2, 55, 57, 59, 75.

[3] Andrieu: *Les Ordines Romani*, Vol. 2, pp. 90, 161.

metal frontals, as well as frontals of painted wood.[1] Metal frontals of gold and silver were also in use in England during the Anglo-Saxon period as well as in the later middle ages after the Norman Conquest at places such as St. Albans, Glastonbury and Croyland Abbeys.[2] Such metal frontals, as well as the painted wooden ones, were detachable, and formed no part of the structure of the altar. The altar itself had little or no decoration or carving on it; so that when it was stripped on Maundy Thursday until Easter Even, it presented an appearance that did not conflict with the nature of the last three days of Holy Week.

In the Eastern Orthodox rite the altar is normally covered with two cloths which serve the same purpose as a frontal. The first of these has reference to the winding-sheet in which the body of Christ was wrapped, and is white, and is known as the *katasarkion*. Hence the altar is Christ in the midst of His church. Over this is placed the silk cloth known as the *endyton, ependysis* or *ephaploma*.[3]

In modern times in some parts of the Roman Catholic Church the vesting of the altar with the *antependium* has been abandoned and the tendency has developed to decorate the altar supports and front with elaborate carving; but this is in conflict with the rubrics of the Roman Missal[4] and the Pontifical. The latter says in the office for the ordering of subdeacons: 'For the altar of Holy Church is Christ Himself, as John bears witness, who, in his Apocalypse, tells us that he beheld a golden altar (*Rev.* viii. 3) set before the throne, on and by which the offerings of the faithful are made acceptable to God the Father. The cloths and corporals of this altar are members of Christ, God's faithful people, with whom, as with costly garments, the Lord is clad, according to the Psalmist "The Lord is King and hath put on glorious apparel." ' (*Ps.* xciii. 1)[5] The great basilicas of St. Peter's, St. Mary Major and St. John Lateran are vested with frontals, both back and front of the altar, except for the last three days of Holy Week.

It cannot be claimed, however, that the custom of having vestments, altar palls and frontals in differing colours for the liturgical seasons is of high antiquity, although its teaching significance and symbolism is of great value. In the Anglo-Saxon era in England and

---

[1] Braun: op. cit., Vol. 2, Plates 131–143.
[2] Rock: op. cit., Vol. 1, pp. 188–9.
[3] A. A. King: op. cit., Vol. 2, p. 113; also Salaville: op. cit., pp. 134–5.
[4] *Missale Romanum* (Tournai, 1950) *Rubricae generales Missalis*, XX, p. xxiii. Pallio quoque ornetur coloris, quoad fieri potest, diei Festo, vel Officio convenientis.
[5] *Pontificale Romanum* (Rome and Turin, 1941), p. 16.

elsewhere purple, sometimes interwoven with gold thread, was the favourite colour for altar palls and vestments.[1] (See also Frontispiece.)

The earliest liturgical colour sequence known to us is that which was in use in the Latin church of the Holy Sepulchre at Jerusalem. This church was served by the Augustinian Canons; and the colour sequence dates from between A.D. 1100 and 1187. It differs considerably from the modern Roman sequence. Perhaps its most radical difference is the use of Black for Christmas and festivals of Our Lady, and Blue for the Epiphany and the Ascension of Christ.[2] In the last quarter of the twelfth century Pope Innocent III in his *De sacro altaris mysterio*, cap. 24, first brings to our notice the familiar White, Red, Violet and Green of the Roman sequence and rite. The colours used in the Sarum and other late medieval uses in England probably derive in part from those in use in Normandy and France, as many of the Sarum customs have strong affinities with those of medieval Rouen and Bec.

Liturgical colour sequences are not employed in the Eastern Orthodox rites to the same degree as in the West, although White and other colours may be used for festivals, Red for Lent, and Black for the Mass of the pre-Sanctified.[3]

That the Church of England intends to keep the ancient custom of the vested and covered altar is clearly shown by Canon 82 of the Canons Ecclesiastical of 1604, which orders the Holy Table to be 'covered, in time of Divine Service, with a carpet of silk or other decent stuff.' That this was duly carried out is evident by a number of these 'carpets' of the seventeenth and eighteenth centuries that are still in existence and by numerous churchwardens' accounts and inventories of the same period.[4]

The type of frontal employed before the Oxford Movement was usually of the 'throw-over' style enveloping the whole altar. It was in fact an unconscious reversion to the older style of pall that was in use in the earlier period before the fourteenth century. There is, therefore, nothing 'Laudian,' 'Jacobean' or 'Carolean' about this kind of altar vesture; and we shall do well to avoid such terms along with other shibboleths such as 'English Altar,' since these things are not the insular peculiarities of the Church within the Provinces of Canterbury and York.

[1] Rock: op. cit., Vol. 1, pp. 210–11.
[2] *Essays on Ceremonial*, ed. V. Staley, pp. 91–3 (Vol. 4, Library of Liturgiology, 1904).
[3] Salaville: op. cit., p. 166; also A. A. King: *The Rites of Eastern Christendom*, Vol. 2, p. 121.
[4] *Hierurgia Anglicana*, ed. V. Staley, Vol. I, pp. 46–110 (1902).

It has, however, been claimed by recent writers that the altar is a table, and therefore its vesting with the proper pall or frontal should be omitted so that it may be seen to be a table. The high antiquity of the custom and the matter of obedience to canonical and rubrical authority apart, it is as well to remember that the table must be clothed for the banquet. An unvested altar lacks significance. If the altar represents Christ in the midst of His Church, as sound liturgical authority and tradition both in East and West insist, it is unfitting that the altar should remain naked and unclothed while the ministers of Christ array themselves in the panoply of cloth of gold, figured brocades and richly coloured damasks.

We have already indicated that in the earlier centuries the altar was usually four-square and thus of limited length. No doubt the fact that it stood under a ciborium with columns contributed to these limitations. These small cube-like altars continued in England even after the Norman Conquest, as we can see in the illustrations of manuscripts belonging to the twelfth and thirteenth centuries.[1] But with the increasing custom of placing portable feretories and reliquaries on the altar, especially in the greater churches, insufficient space was found on the top of the small altar. Also from the twelfth century it became the custom in some places to set a cross on the altar[2] and one or two candlesticks,[3] although there was no rigid uniformity in this matter. Whereas in the earlier centuries nothing was permitted to stand on the mensa apart from the sacred vessels and the Book of the Gospels, which represented Christ, in the second part of the middle ages, relics of all kinds, together with statuettes in gold and silver, and also numerous altar vessels came to be displayed on the altar on great festivals.[4] Most of the great churches had a Feast of the Relics in the later middle ages.

In the late middle ages and the early period of the Renaissance candlesticks were not left on the altar as a permanent feature apart from their use in the liturgy. Thus Burchard in his *Ordo* of 1502 directs the server to place two lighted candles on the altar before low Mass, but at the end of the rite they are to be extinguished and taken back to the sacristy.[5]

---

[1] See illustrations in *Pictures of Fifty Gothic Altars*, ed. P. Dearmer (1910).
[2] Pocknee: *Cross and Crucifix*, p. 37 (1962).
[3] D. R. Dendy: *The Use of Lights in Christian Worship*, pp. 45–71 (1959).
[4] D. Rock: *Church of our Fathers*, Vol. 3, p. 390 (1905); also see illustration facing p. 42 in J. Perkins: *Westminster Abbey*, Vol. 1 (1938).
[5] J. W. Legg: *Tracts on the Mass* (1904, H.B.S., Vol. 27), pp. 133, 169, 173.

D

Once the canopy ceased to be supported directly on its columns, the lengthening of the altar against a screen or wall became common and produced the 'buffet' type of altar in which the mensa is increasingly treated as a kind of sideboard to support cross, candlesticks, reliquaries and displays of church plate.

2

Side Altars and their Multiplication

IN the primitive era of Christianity every church building possessed but one altar and there was normally only one celebration of the Eucharist on Sundays and other days. The gathering together of the *ecclesia* was an act of unity and fellowship in the Lord's Cross and Resurrection. The multiplication of altars and services would have struck at this unity in Christ. Thus St. Ignatius of Antioch (d. *c.* A.D. 110) writes in the fourth chapter of his epistle to the Philadelphians: 'Take great care to keep one Eucharist. For there is one flesh of our Lord Jesus Christ and one cup to unite us by his blood, one altar (θυσιαστήριον), as there is one bishop, together with the presbytery and the deacons, my fellow-servants.' In North Africa the custom of having only one altar in a church continued until the seventh century when the Moslem invasion virtually extinguished Christianity.[1]

In the Eastern Orthodox Church and the lesser Eastern Churches this custom of the one altar is still maintained. But there are sometimes oratories or chapels loosely connected with, or outside, the main church building, known as παρεκκλησίαι, where votive offices may be celebrated on week days; but the single altar remains in the church properly so called and there are no side chapels.[2]

In the Latin West, however, there was a gradual but increasing declension from the primitive ideal, both in regard to the number of altars and the number of Masses that could be celebrated in one day.

In Rome from about the sixth century, oratories in honour of the Apostles and other martyrs, along with the altars relating to them, which had been scattered all over the city, came to be erected inside the churches. From the sixth epistle of Pope Gregory the Great we learn that about A.D. 590 Bishop Palladius of Saintes had a church built with thirteen altars in it.[3] From that time onwards the increase of altars becomes common. Three causes may be said to have contributed to this increase:

(*a*) The cultus of the saints and their relics which could best be observed in connexion with a special altar;

[1] Braun: op. cit., Vol. 1, p. 373.   [2] Salaville: *Eastern Liturgies*, p. 114.
[3] P.L., Tome 77, 834.

(b) The increasing desire on the part of priests and congregations for votive Masses with a special intention, e.g. for a wedding, a birthday, for the anniversary of an ordination and for departed friends and relatives. Examples of these and other votive Masses are to be found in the so-called Leonine[1] and Gelasian Sacramentaries, which are certainly not later than the sixth century;[2]

(c) It was forbidden for a priest to use an altar that had already been used by a bishop on the same day; and it was the normal practice until about the ninth century for an altar to be used but once each day.[3] Such limitations were bound to lead to an increase in the number of altars in a church as the desire for frequent votive and requiem Masses increased.

By the ninth century every large church in the West had a considerable number of side altars.[4] The famous monastic church of St. Gall, designed about 820, had, besides two altars in the nave, an altar both in the eastern and western apses, and four altars, both in the north and south aisles, all of which were orientated.[5] In the tenth century an attempt was made by episcopal and synodical decrees to stem this increase in the too frequent celebration of the Eucharist; and in the eleventh and thirteenth centuries more than one Pope tried to forbid the duplication or bination of Masses on any one day.[6]

But in the thirteenth century the growth of the number of priests in the larger cities, together with the increasing admonition that all priests must say Mass daily (an admonition quite unknown in the earlier centuries), led to a new increase in the number of side altars. Churches with thirty to forty-five altars were not exceptional.[7] Church architecture had to be adapted to this increase in side altars. The north and south aisles of the nave had their outer walls pierced and opened out, as at Chichester Cathedral, to accommodate new altars and chapels; and the building east of the High altar in England, known as the retro-choir, was adapted for new altars, usually with an easternmost altar in honour of the Blessed Virgin Mary.

Then, too, the chantry chapel, usually containing the tomb of a celebrity, was a prominent feature of the late middle ages. One of the most celebrated of these is the chapel of Henry VII and his queen

---

[1] L. C. Mohlberg: *Sacramentarium Veronense* (Rome, 1956), pp. 139–41.
[2] H. A. Wilson: *The Gelasian Sacramentary* (1894), pp. 245–313; also A. Chavasse: *Le Sacramentaire Gélasien* (Tournai, 1958), pp. 478–95.
[3] Braun: Vol. 1, pp. 368–73.   [4] Braun: Vol. 1, pp. 373–7.
[5] Conant: *Carolingian and Romanesque Architecture*, pp. 20–2.
[6] Jungmann: *Mass of the Roman Rite*, Vol. 1, p. 223.
[7] Braun: Vol. 1, pp. 378–82.

at Westminster. Here a magnificent new building was projected east of the main structure of the Abbey.[1] At Winchester Cathedral the retro-choir still has more than one chantry chapel and altar built for the saying of a requiem Mass on appointed occasions for the former Bishops of Winchester who are buried there.

In France the apsidal east end, a feature usually absent from English cathedral and parish churches, was enlarged into an ambulatory round and behind the High altar. From the outer wall of the ambulatory there radiated a series of absidoles containing altars, the whole arrangement being known as the 'chevet.' An early example of the chevet with its chapels is that of the Church of St. Martin at Tours, built between 903 and 918.[2]

A feature of parochial life in England and elsewhere in the late middle ages, which contributed to the increase in side altars, was the parish and craft guilds. The guilds and confraternities had a religious foundation and usually bore the name of a saint or of some theological mystery, such as the Holy Trinity, the Ascension, or Corpus Christi. Cities such as London, York, Norwich and Bristol had many of these guilds; and indeed they also existed even in country parishes.[3] Such guilds often had their own priest-chaplain who said Mass at the guild altar on certain occasions in the year as well as a requiem on the death of a member. The guild also equipped and maintained an altar in the chapel of a cathedral or parish church. Thus the company of Armourers of the City of London formed a guild about 1388 'to burn a wax light to the praise and honour of the famous martyr (St. George) in his chapel within the cathedral church of St. Paul and charitably maintained, and continued certain divine services and ecclesiastical ornaments.'[4] In 1389 in the parish church of St. Botolph at Boston there was added a new chapel in honour of St. Peter and St. Paul, built by the confraternity of that name, who also maintained two chaplains.[5] Many more instances could be given of guilds having their own altar and chapel, either in cathedrals or parish churches, thus increasing the number of side altars in almost every church in the land during the fourteenth and fifteenth centuries.

It has been the theme of writers, both Catholic and Protestant, during the last half century, that the late middle ages was a time of

---

[1] J. Perkins: *Westminster Abbey, its worship and ornaments* (1940), Vol. 2, pp. 154–70.
[2] Conant: op. cit., p. 28.
[3] For a list of English guilds, see H. F. Westlake: *The Parish Gilds of Mediaeval England* (1919), pp. 137–238.
[4] Westlake: op. cit., pp. 23–4.   [5] Ibid., p. 157.

decline in theology and Christian worship in the West. An excessive individualism characterized church life and is reflected in the vast increase in votive and requiem Masses, in which the needs and anxieties of individuals found an outlet. Such needs can never be ignored or forgotten in the life of the church. On the other hand society has a high worth and the ideal of a single altar and the single Eucharist expressed in the words of St. Ignatius of Antioch, which we have already quoted, should always be borne in mind. In our own day liturgical reform manifested in the Parish Communion and the emphasis on the Church as the Body of Christ which offers the sacrifice of Christ and His Church must be reflected, both in the planning of church buildings, and in the conduct of the liturgy.

3

The Altar Canopy and its Veils

It is not until the fourth century that we encounter evidence for the erection of a canopy over the altar. Some have thought the custom was derived from the erection of such canopies supported on columns over tombs in cemeteries; and where a saint was buried under the altar the transference of the custom would be obvious. It is also possible that the custom of erecting a canopy over the throne of the Emperor may have had some influence since the altar came to be regarded as the throne of Christ to which reverence was paid. While others have thought the altar canopy is derived from pagan sources. Thus St. John Chrysostom (d. A.D. 407) in his forty-second homily speaks of the little temples or shrines which Demetrius the silversmith made in honour of Diana of the Ephesians (*Acts* xix. 24–25), and which he likens to ciboria.[1]

The terms used to denote this feature of the altar have tended to vary according to its form and the materials employed. The term *canopy* derives from κωνωπεῖον, which meant a cover above a bed supporting veils which reached down to the bed to keep off the mosquito or κώνωψ.

As we have already stated, it is in the fourth century that we first find evidence for the altar canopy. It was supported on four columns or piers, and was four-square in plan, covering both the altar and its foot-pace. It was made of stone, marble, wood or metal. The wooden structures were seldom left without a metal covering. The most usual material was stone or marble. But the canopy presented by Constantine the Great (d. 337) to the Lateran basilica was of silver, since it is described in the *Liber Pontificalis* as *fastigium argenteum battutile*.[2] This canopy was on a magnificent scale; but it only lasted until the fifth century when it was carried away by the Visigoths and replaced by one less magnificent given by Pope Sixtus III. Other terms for the canopy surmounted on four columns or piers were *ciborium* and *umbraculum*. The term ciborium is thought to be derived from the Greek κιβώριον, which originally meant the hollow seed-case of the Egyptian water lily (*nymphaea nelumbo*), and the term came to be used to describe a drinking-cup because of its resemblance to the seed-case. But in

[1] P.G., Tome 60, 297.
[2] L. Duchesne: *Le Liber Pontificalis*, p. 172, Vol. 1 (Paris, 1886).

Christian worship the term ciborium means the canopy with its dome over the altar; and only in the middle ages does the term also come to be applied to a vessel with a cover for containing altar breads or hosts.[1]

According to Braun the first evidence for the use of the term 'ciborium' in connexion with the altar is in the life of Pope Symmachus (498–514); but the word is there spelt 'tiburium,' since the Pope is described as setting up a *tiburium ex argento purissimo* in the rotunda of St. Andrew by St. Peter's, and also in the basilica of St. Martin.[2]

In the East the first reference to the ciborium seems to be in the History of Armenia by Lazarus of Pharp, written at the end of the fifth or the beginning of the sixth century. In this is described a vision of the Catholicos Isaac (403–438) in which on a *bema* (sanctuary) made of clouds he saw a tent-like ciborium (tetraskel), which was furnished with a cupola, made of pure gold and covered with a white awning. On the roof was set a cross and under it stood a four-sided table decorated with many coloured jewels on which lay a host and a bunch of grapes.[3]

In the sixth century Paul the Silentiary uses the term πύργος, a tower, to describe the canopy over the altar of the Church of the Holy Wisdom at Constantinople.[4]

No complete ciboria have been preserved from the earlier centuries. The most notable collection of ciboria, that is of canopies mounted or supported on columns, is to be found in the churches of Central and Northern Italy. The earliest one remaining in its original position dates from A.D. 812, and is in one of the aisles of Sant' Apollinare in Classe, Ravenna. Other well-known examples include San Clemente, Rome, 1118, St. Lawrence outside the walls, 1148, Santa Maria in Cosmedin, 1296, St. John Lateran, fourteenth century, Sant' Ambrogio, Milan, twelfth century, with columns of the fourth century. Earlier than these examples is the altar and ciborium at Castel Sant' Elia near Nepi with its foot-pace on the nave side of the altar. (See Plate 1.) This dates from the tenth century.

Following on the mission of St. Augustine to Britain in A.D. 597 the Anglo-Saxon Church had a fairly close affinity with Rome; and evidence exists that in the pre-Conquest era altars in this land were

---

[1] W. H. Freestone: *The Sacrament Reserved*, pp. 207–8 (1917).
[2] J. Braun: *Der christliche Altar*, Vol. 2, pp. 189–91 (Munich, 1924), also Duchesne, op. cit., Vol. 1, p. 261.
[3] Braun: op. cit., Vol. 2, pp. 194–5.   [4] D.A.C.L., Tome 3, 1604.

cube-shaped and surmounted by ciboria as we can see in some of the illustrations in the *Benedictional of St. Ethelwold*. But no evidence exists to suggest that during the Anglo-Saxon period it was customary for the celebrant to face the people when saying mass, although the altar was free-standing. Most Anglo-Saxon churches had the altar at the east end, and not at the west end as in the Roman basilicas. The illustrations in Ethelwold's *Benedictional* show the celebrant on the nave side of the altar (see Frontispiece). In the Life of St. Wilfrid (d. 709) by Eddius Stephanus there is a description of the consecration of the Church of Ripon in 670 by the saint, in which we are told: 'Then St. Wilfrid the bishop stood in front of the altar, and turning to the people in the presence of the kings, read out clearly a list of the consecrated places etc.'[1]

As late as the second half of the twelfth century we find evidence in England for the use of the ciborium over the altar, since in *The Magdalen Pontifical* provision is made for a canopy over the altar in the rite for the dedication of a church under *Prefatio ciborii id est umbracula altaris*.[2] The Pontifical of Durandus, compiled about 1294, for use in France, provides for the consecration of an altar with a ciborium.[3]

In the late middle ages, from the fourteenth century onwards, we find an adapted form of the ciborium introduced to meet the changed conditions where the altar came to be placed close to an altar screen or an east wall with a large window. The Roman basilica seldom had a window in the apse, and the altar stood on the chord of the apse and was free-standing, but in Northern Europe where daylight was a primary consideration, the large and low East window was developed. In these conditions the ciborium standing on its heavy columns proved an obstruction; and so the posts were retained around the altar, but usually in a much slenderer form; while the canopy proper was raised above the window and suspended from the roof, and in this form is known as a *Tester*. The canopy was usually four-square, thus covering the foot-pace and the altar. A tester hung over the High altar at Westminster Abbey in the late middle ages, as we can see from one of the illustrations in the Islip Roll.[4] But examples also exist where the tester was curved or raised round the east window such as at Clun and Ludlow, where canopies still remain *in situ*. The tester was generally made of wood and gilded and decorated. (See Plate 11.) In other

[1] B. Colgrave: *The Life of Bishop Wilfrid*, Chap. 17 (Cambridge, 1927).
[2] H. A. Wilson: *The Magdalen Pontifical*, p. 133 (H.B.S., Vol. 39, 1910).
[3] M. Andrieu: *Le Pontifical Romain*, Tome 3, p. 531.
[4] See illustration facing page 50, J. Perkins, *Westminster Abbey*, Vol. 1 (1938).

instances instead of a tester the roof over the altar was boarded-in and treated with carved wooden motifs and coloured.[1]

The posts surrounding the altar were also of wood, although instances are known of them being made of metal,[2] and they were sometimes surmounted by carved and gilded angels holding tapers. Between the posts were suspended the riddel curtains on rods. This arrangement has come to be termed, somewhat inaccurately and misleadingly, an 'English Altar.' There is nothing peculiarly English or insular about it as evidence exists for this arrangement in various parts of Northern Europe; and it is known to have been in existence in French churches and cathedrals as late as the eighteenth century, e.g. Auxerre Cathedral. (See also Plate 24.) It is also likely that this arrangement was at one time in use in some Spanish churches as more than one example of a separate tester is extant in that country. (See Plate 6.) The High altar of Gerona Cathedral is an important example of the transitional stage between the ciborium and the riddel-post type of altar.[3] At Gerona the fourteenth-century canopy still rests on its posts, although these are much more slender than the stone columns or piers of the ciborium. (See Plate 7.)

In England the ciborium was still in evidence in the sixteenth century as we know from the beautiful example erected by Torrigiano over the altar of the chapel of Henry VII at Westminster. This remained *in situ* until it was destroyed by the Puritans during the Great Rebellion. Since 1935 a copy of Torrigiano's ciborium has been restored in this chapel.[4] (See Plate 8.)

Something must be said in regard to the term variously spelt *baldachino*, *baldachinum* or *baldaquin*. This term is often used somewhat loosely to describe any canopy over an altar. It should, however, be applied to a canopy made from a woven fabric, and not to wooden, stone or metal canopies. Baldachino is derived from the Italian *Baldacco*, meaning Bagdad, where the textile for such canopies with a silk woof and metal thread was first made. This type of canopy made of fabric appears in the Renaissance period, and particularly where the altar was attached or close to a wall. (See Plate 9.) The *Caerimonale Episcoporum* of the Roman rite says: 'If the altar is attached to a wall . . . high above it should be hung a canopy, which they call a baldaquin,

---

[1] F. E. Howard and F. H. Crossley: *English Church Woodwork*, pp. 138–9 (2nd ed., 1927); also F. Bond: *The Chancel of English Churches*, pp. 21–6 (1916).
[2] See J. W. Legg: *Some Principles and Services of the Prayer Book historically considered* (1899), pp. 6 and 12.
[3] Braun: op. cit., Vol. 2, p. 233.
[4] J. Perkins: *Westminster Abbey, its worship and ornaments* (1940), Vol. 2, pp. 207–9.

square in shape covering the altar and its foot-pace, of the colour of the rest of the vestments.'[1] The difficulty and inconvenience connected with the changing of this type of canopy to match the liturgical colours means that in practice only two baldaquins are used in many instances, one for general use and one for penitential occasions.

Canopies did not cease to be erected in England after the Reformation. An example may be seen in St. Mary Woolnoth in the City of London erected by Nicholas Hawksmoor in 1727. (See Plate 10.) Nineteenth-century examples are to be seen over the High altars of Lincoln and Peterborough Cathedrals. In the twentieth century outstanding examples of ciboria have been erected to the designs of the late Sir Ninian Comper at Aberdeen Cathedral, St. Mary's, Wellingborough, and Pusey House Chapel, Oxford. Admiration for the magnificent new ciborium over the High altar of St. Paul's Cathedral must be tempered with regret that neither the altar itself, nor its cross and candlesticks, are in accord with sound liturgical tradition nor with the Canon Law of the Church of England.

Recent commentators have tended to draw too sharp a contrast between the liturgy as performed in the Roman basilicas with its alleged 'openness,' and the hieratic and veiled liturgy of the Eastern rites. But these divergent tendencies have only become most evident since the last part of the middle ages and the Renaissance in the West. As we shall show in another part of this work the solid screen or *iconostasis* of the Eastern rites today is a much later develpment than is commonly supposed.

The first reference to the veil before the altar in patristic writings is not from Syria but from North Africa. It is found in a letter written by Synesius of Cyrene about A.D. 410 to Theophilus of Alexandria; in which he speaks of 'the table of the Holy Communion and the mystic veil' (τὸ καταπέτασμα μυστικόν) becoming the instruments of an attack by the Arians.[2] It will be noted that the term καταπέτασμα employed by Synesius for the veil is the same as that used by the writers of the Gospels to describe the veil of the Temple in the holy of holies at Jerusalem, e.g. Matthew xxvii. 51. But the first definite evidence for the veiling of the altar during the liturgy comes to us from the East in a homily by St. John Chrysostom (d. 407), who writes: 'When the sacrifice is brought forth, and Christ, the Lord's sheep, is sacrificed; when thou hearest the words "Let us all pray together," when thou

---

[1] *Caerimoniale Episcoporum*, p. 73 (Rome, 1606).
[2] P.G., Tome 66, 1420.

beholdest the curtains drawn aside, then think that heaven is parted and the angels are descending.'[1]

Whatever may have been the custom during the fourth century in Syria, it seems necessary to point out that the veil or curtain is not drawn to obscure the altar in the present Byzantine liturgy except at two points (and only two), and these occasions seem to have nothing to do with awe, fear or mystery. The veil is drawn for the litany at the laying-out of the gifts, after the Great Entrance, because at an earlier time several patens and chalices were offered; and the movements to and fro of the deacons at the altar were found a hindrance to devotion and a distraction from the litany that was in progress at the same time.

The second time the veil is drawn is at 'Holy Things for the holy,'[2] when the chalices were being mixed with water before the communion, and there was also the same kind of 'va-et-vient' in the sanctuary. Hence the curtain is drawn until the chalices are mixed and the communicating clergy have completed their double circuit round the altar to receive under two species. Indeed, when a bishop celebrates the Byzantine liturgy, the veil is not drawn on the first of these two occasions, and thus the altar remains visible right up to 'Holy Things for the holy.' Far too late in fact for ideas of fear and awe which a number of commentators have supposed is the sole reason for this action in the Eastern rites!

In the West the veiling of the altar has been the subject of considerable differences of opinion amongst scholars; and the matter is still somewhat obscure. We bring to the notice of our readers the inventory of church furnishings and ornaments that is contained in the *Charta Cornutiana*, a document compiled about A.D. 471; and which refers to a church at Tivoli outside Rome. It cannot be ignored that in the section following on references to chalices and patens there is a considerable list of cloths and veils, several of which are of coloured silk. Thus, two items are: *Vela tramosirica leuchoporphoria* II and *Vela olosirica coccoprasina* II.[3]

More definite evidence comes to us in the *Liber Pontificalis* during the seventh and eighth centuries at Rome. This evidence leaves no

[1] Ep. ad. Ephes., P.G., Tome 62, 29.
[2] *The Divine Liturgy of St. John Chrysostom*, 3rd ed. (Faith Press N.D.), pp. 51–2; also F. E. Brightman: *Liturgies Eastern and Western*, pp. 590–1 (1896); also *Service Book of the Holy Orthodox-Catholic Apostolic Church*, p. 114 (New York, 1922).
[3] D.A.C.L., Tome 3, 882.

doubt that at that time curtains or veils were suspended round the ciboria of the great Roman basilicas; and that the altar must have had veils on all four sides of the ciborium is not in doubt since the term 'tetravela' is used in more than one instance. Thus Pope Sergius (687–701) gave to St. Peter's eight veils, four of white and four of scarlet.[1] Pope John VI (701–5) gave a set of altar veils to the Church of St. Paul outside the walls.[2] While Pope Leo III (795–816) gave several sets of veils to the Lateran basilica and St. Paul's outside the walls which were in various colours and were, in some instances, decorated with jewels and pearls.[3] It is necessary to observe that the use of the term *tetravela* in these examples in the *Liber Pontificalis* implies Greek influence. During the seventh and eighth centuries there was a considerable colony of Greeks and Syrians at Rome, and more than one Pope of that period is known to have been of Greek or Syrian origin. It may be, therefore, that the veiling of the altar at Rome was introduced through their influence. There seems to be no evidence in the *Ordines Romani* of that period as to when the veils were drawn.[4]

At the present time, the rods for holding the veils may be seen *in situ* on all four sides of a number of Italian ciboria, e.g. San Clemente in Cassauria, Abruzzi, and on the two side altars at Terracina Cathedral, as well as at Anagni Cathedral and at Castel Sant' Elia, near Nepi, in Central Italy. (See Plates 1 and 2.) In Northern Europe veils were undoubtedly employed round the ciboria as we can see in a number of illustrations that accompany manuscripts such as the *Benedictional of Ethelwold* and the *Utrecht Psalter;*[5] also on occasions the columns of the canopy were wreathed with garlands of evergreens and flowers.[6] Evidence that the curtain or veil was drawn before the altar is to be found in more than one of the Anglo-Saxon Pontificals which belong to the late tenth century, such as the *Pontifical of Egbert* and the *Alet Pontifical*, in connexion with the rite of consecration of the altar by

---

[1] Duchesne: op. cit., Vol. 1, p. 373. Hic fecit (Sergius) in circuitu altaris basilicae tetravela VIII, quatuor ex albis et quatuor a coccino.

[2] Ibid., p. 383. In basilica beati Pauli Apostoli inter columnas altaris dextra aevaque vela alba.

[3] Ibid., Vol. 2, p. 29. Praeclarus pontifex fecit in circuitu altaris tetravela rubea olosirica alitina, habentes tabulas seu orbiclos de chrisoclabo, diversis depictos historiis cum stellis de chrisoclabo; necnon et in medio cruces de chrisoclabo ex margaretis ornatas mire magnitudinis et pulchritudinis decorata, quae in diebus festis ibidem ad decorem mittuntur. Pari modo ubi supra fecit et alia tetravila alaba oloserica rosata paschatiles, habentes tabulas atque orbiclos de chrisoclabo, necnon et cruces cum chrisoclabo ex margeretis ornatas, cum periclisis de chrisoclabo. Immo etiam et alia vela modica IIII, ubi supra, in singulis columnis de ciborio fecit, habentes tigris de chrisoclabo, et in circuitu ornatas de blati. Verum etiam et alia vela IIII, eadem habentes similitudinem in basilica doctoris mundi beati Pauli apostoli in columnis de ciborio posuit.

[4] See texts in M. Andrieu, *Les Ordines Romani*, Vol. 2 (1948).

[5] See illustrations facing p. 2 in J. D. Chambers: *Divine Worship in England* (New ed., 1877).

[6] D. Rock: *The Church of our Fathers*, pp. 155–6, Vol. 1.

the bishop thus: *Venientes autem ante altare et extenso velo inter eos et populum, facit episcopus crucem de sancto chrismate.*[1] The veiling of the sanctuary at the consecration of the altar also appears in the ninth and tenth centuries in France.[2]

The introduction of the new ceremony of the Elevation of the Host in the West in the thirteenth century[3] meant the altar could not be veiled during the Canon or Eucharistic Prayer, since it was essential that the uplifted Host should be seen by the worshippers. But a relic of the veiling of the altar in Northern Europe persisted in the use of the Lenten veil drawn across the sanctuary during the forty days of the fast. Its use was not confined to England since it was known in Germany as the 'Fastenvelum.' It was only drawn aside at the reading of the Gospel at High Mass on Sundays. Indeed, evidence is now available that the veiling of the sanctuary has continued in places during the present century. Examples have been noted at Seville, Majorca and in Calabria in Italy[4] as well as Sicily. It also continues to be the custom in the Armenian Church during Lent.[5]

Some doubt has been cast on the authenticity of these facts by the late Dom Gregory Dix,[6] but there can be no doubt that this custom was widely observed during Lent, as winches, pulleys and hooks in a number of English medieval churches still testify.[7] It has further been suggested that the veiling of the altar and sanctuary has been confused with the veiling of the Crucifix and the attendant figures of Our Lady and St. John on the Rood Screen. But this is disproved by references to inventories which include veils for the Rood and the sanctuary. Thus at St. Martin, Outwich, London, there was in 1547 'A clothe called the Vale And a clothe called the roode Clothe steyned.'[8]

The custom of veiling crucifixes, statues and pictures during the whole of Lent, that is during the forty days, can probably be traced back to the tenth century.[9] At that time Christ was depicted on the Cross as alive and triumphant rather than in the anguish of death,[10]

---

[1] *The Pontifical of Egbert*, ed. W. Greenwell, pp. 45–6 (Surtees Soc., Vol. 27, 1853); also E. Martène, *De Antiquis Ecclesiae Ritibus*, Vol. 2, p. 254 (Antwerp, 1736–8).
[2] L. Duchesne: *Christian Worship*, p. 413 (5th ed., 1923).
[3] J. A. Jungmann: *The Mass of the Roman Rite*, Vol. 1, p. 118.
[4] J. N. Comper: *Further Thoughts on the English Altar*, p. 49 (1932).
[5] A. A. King: *Rites of Eastern Christendom*, Vol. 2, p. 569.
[6] G. Dix: *The Shape of the Liturgy*, p. 482 (1945).
[7] J. N. Comper: op. cit., p. 49; see also H. J. Feasey, *Ancient Holy Week Ceremonial*, pp. 13–31 (1897).
[8] H. B. Walters: *London Churches at the Reformation*, p. 392 (1939).
[9] Braun: op. cit., Vol. 2, 148–9.
[10] Pocknee: *Cross and Crucifix* (1962), pp. 21–2.

while statues of the Saints were intended to reflect their heavenly glory. To veil these things during the penitential season of Lent seemed fitting and appropriate. The custom of veiling the crucifix only from the fifth Sunday in Lent, commonly called Passion Sunday, appears to have developed in the seventeenth century.[1]

[1] Jungmann: *Public Worship* (1957), p. 185.

4

Altar Screens

(a) *Before the altar*

The separation of the altar and the sanctuary from the nave or body of the church has been a recognized custom from the fourth century onwards. Prior to the Peace of the Church under Constantine the Great (d. 337), the ceremonial details of Christian worship are scanty and uncertain in many respects. Eusebius of Caesarea in his *Vita Constantini* describes the sanctuary of the Church of the Apostles erected by Constantine at Constantinople as enclosed by screens or lattice-work. The same writer in his *Ecclesiastical History* (Bk. 10, ch. 4) speaks of the Church at Tyre, rebuilt by the Emperor *circa* 314, thus: 'For when he had completed the temple, he adorned it with lofty thrones in honour of those who preside, and also with seats decently arranged in order throughout the whole, and after all these things he hath placed in the midst, the holy of holies even the altar, and again surrounded this part also, that the multitude might not tread thereon, with a fence of wooden lattice-work delicately wrought with the craftsman's utmost skill.'[1]

Much has been made in recent years of the alleged 'all-seeing' principle of the Roman basilica in contrast to the screening of the sanctuary in the present Eastern rites.[2] But these divergences in their present forms are of comparatively late growth. The screening of the altar described by Eusebius at Constantinople and Tyre did not mean that a solid screen or *iconostasis* had been erected. Indeed, Dix was mistaken when he supposed that a solid screen was built in front of the altar of the Church of the Holy Wisdom at Constantinople by Justinian the Great in A.D. 537.[3] (See Plate 13(*a*).)

It is incorrect and misleading, therefore, to use the term *iconostasis* to describe any of the screens in Eastern Christendom during the first millennium of the Christian church. On the other hand, it is equally misleading to suggest that screens of some kind were not in use in the great Roman basilicas in the earlier centuries. Most of these churches were considerably altered in the late middle ages and in the baroque period, and the largest of them, St. Peter's in the Vatican, was completely demolished. It is when we come to study the plans and pictures

[1] J. E. L. Oulton and H. J. Lawlor: *Eusebius, The Ecclesiastical History*, Vol. 2, pp. 426–7 (1932).
[2] G. Dix: *The Shape of the Liturgy*, pp. 480–2 (1945).
[3] Ibid., p. 481.

PLATE 17

THE APOGEE OF ITALIAN BAROQUE

The altar in the Chapel of St. Ignatius Loyola in the Church of Il Gesù, Rome, designed by Andrea Pozzo (1642–1709).

The altar itself has become a pediment or base to support a vast and towering architectural edifice in honour of Ignatius, whose statue appears as the central motif. The vestiges of the altar ciborium now form a frame for the whole setting.

PLATE 18

AN ENGLISH MEDIEVAL REREDOS

Given by Bishop Despenser to Norwich Cathedral about 1381, this retable depicts the scourging, bearing the Cross, the Crucifixion, Resurrection and the Ascension of Christ. The style of painting together with the use of gold and gesso show the East Anglian tradition. The frame of the reredos is decorated chiefly with the symbols of the Passion.

Used as a table after the Reformation, this altar-piece is now the reredos in the Chapel of St. Luke on the south side of the Cathedral Ambulatory.

66

PLATE 19 THE SYRIAN LITURGICAL PLAN

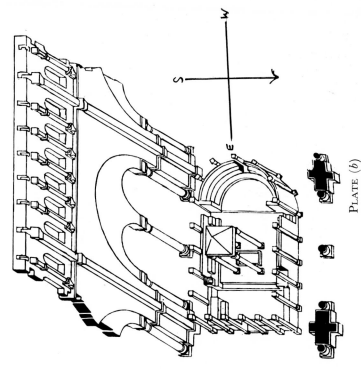

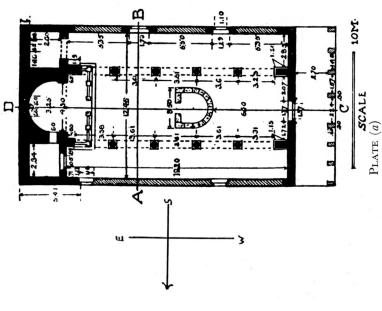

SCALE |———————| 10M.

PLATE (a)

This plan shows the lay-out of the church at Karab-chemps as reconstructed by H. C. Butler. The horseshoe-like chancel with seats for the bishop and his assistants is mid-way down the nave. For the first part of the liturgy the bishop sat or stood here facing east.

PLATE (b)

An isometric sectional drawing of the ambon and horse-shoe chancel at St. Sergius, Rosafa, as reconstructed by G. Tchalenko. The bishop's seat is in the middle of the inverted apse. The lections were read at the ambon, which has a canopy over it. At the same time of the offertory the bishop and his ministers left the chancel and advanced to the altar further east, where they stood with their backs to the congregation for the Eucharistic Prayer.

67

PLATE 20

A German Triptych

This type of reredos came into fashion in the last part of the middle ages, notably in Germany and the Low Countries. This example, made in the sixteenth century, comes from North Germany, possibly Hamburg. Decorated in gilt and polychrome, it depicts the life and martyrdom of St. Margaret of Antioch in the third century. Some of the events are legendary; and the absence of any reference to Christ and the fundamental doctrines of the Christian religion will be noted.

PLATE 21

A RUSSIAN ICONOSTASIS

This type of solid screen, covered entirely with icons and pictures, only developed in the East in the second part of the middle ages; it is Russian rather than Byzantine in origin.

Behind the central or Royal doors, which are closed in this picture, stands the cube-shaped altar. At the time of the administration of Holy Communion the celebrant and his assistants come outside the screen and give the sacrament to the people who stand and not kneel for this act.

PLATE 22

FOUR MEDIEVAL PYXES

Made of copper with Champlevé enamel in the thirteenth century at Limoges. These pyxes were intended for the reservation of the Blessed Sacrament, which was usually in one kind.

PLATE 23

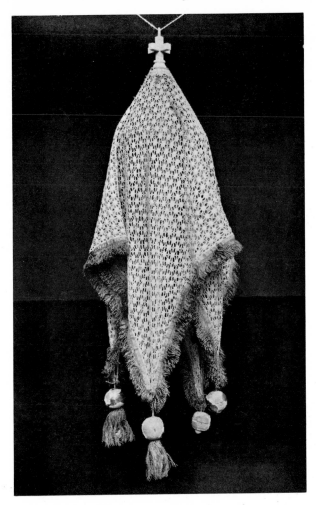

AN ENGLISH PYX-CLOTH

The only extant example of the pre-Reformation cloth or canopy in England, belonging to Hessett Church, Suffolk (and now in the British Museum). It is square in form, measuring on each side, two feet five and a half inches; made of linen worked into a pattern resembling lace by drawing and knotting some of the threads. Around the edge is a fringe in rose and yellow with gilt balls and tassels of silk at each corner.

PLATE 24

A French Renaissance Altar

From an engraving in the *Caerimoniale Parisiense*, 1703, this picture shows the restraint at this late date in the appointments of the altar that were still to be found in France. No candlesticks remain on the altar outside divine service. The Eucharist is reserved in a dove suspended in a cone-shaped canopy over the altar.

PLATE 25

A Spanish Hanging Pyx

This picture is an illustration in the second volume of the *Constitutiones Palatinae*, made in 1337 for the King of Majorca, James II.

The hanging pyx in the form of a cup or ciborium is contained in a carved wooden tower of Gothic design which is suspended over the altar. In the apse is a cupboard or aumbry holding some books. After presenting his offering the king kneels and kisses the celebrant's stole.

PLATE 26

A Eucharistic Dove

Made of copper-gilt with enamels in gold, blue and yellow with turquoise and topaz stones. It is the best-preserved example of this form of eucharistic pyx. Made in the twelfth century it belongs to Salzburg Cathedral, Austria.

PLATE 27

A Spanish Pyx

A renaissance pyx in silver. Parcel-gilt of the sixteenth century. Designed for the reservation of the Blessed Sacrament when enclosed in a tabernacle.

PLATE 28

TERRACINA CATHEDRAL, ITALY

A rare example of a basilica retaining altars with ciboria to the aisles as well as the nave. The
church faces west. The confessio under one of the side altars will be noted. Since this photograph
was made the temporary flight of wooden steps on the nave side of the High altar have been removed;
and the celebrant now faces east at all three altars when he celebrates *versus populum*. The general
structure of the church belongs to the twelfth century.

PLATE 29

MODERN ROMAN CATHOLIC ALTARS

In the Church of Our Lady of Peace, Braintree, and designed by Mr. Geoffrey Webb. The High altar conforms strictly to the rubrics of the Roman Missal and *Caerimoniale*. The tabernacle for the reservation of the Blessed Sacrament is completely enveloped with the tent-like veil. The ciborium covers the foot-pace as well as the altar.

PLATE 30

CONTEMPORARY AND LITURGICAL

The new Church of St. Katherine, Hammersmith, reflects the trend of liturgical reform, yet is in the mainstream of tradition. The altar has only a small pair of candlesticks on it; the cross on the east wall renders one standing on the altar unnecessary. The altar is vested in accordance with the law of the Church of England, and the altar linen comes well down at the ends of the altar. Over the altar there is a canopy whose area covers the foot-pace as well as the mensa. Symbols from early Christian art, such as the fish, the dove and the anchor-cross, form part of its decoration.

PLATE 31

A RIDDEL POST ALTAR

Made to the designs of the late F. E. Howard in the English Gothic tradition, this altar and reredos in Tring Parish Church reproduce, in a medieval setting with the low east window, the type of altar that developed in the late middle ages in England and other parts of Northern Europe.

PLATE 32

THE LITURGICAL ALTAR

Designed in 1940 by the late Sir Ninian Comper for the Cathedral Church of St. Andrew, Aberdeen, this altar and its canopy exemplify how the chief ornament of Christian worship should be appointed. The Reserved Sacrament is suspended in a pyx over the altar.

of old St. Peter's (see Plate 12), we realize that the difference between the earlier Byzantine screens and those in the old Roman basilicas has been greatly exaggerated. (See Plate 13(*b*).)

There is every reason to believe that the altar-screen in old St. Peter's was originally erected in the time of Constantine the Great, although it may have been altered by the addition of a second row of columns in the eighth century.[1]

In principle this type of screen had a wainscotting of marble between four and five feet in height, with an opening in the midst before the altar. On the top of this were a series of porphyry columns supporting an architrave or entablature of marble. From this architrave, and sometimes also from the vault of the altar canopy, there were suspended votive lamps containing perfumed oil, which burnt in honour of the saint whose body lay under the altar. Paulinus of Nola (d. 431) in one of his poems which he wrote in honour of his Patron, St. Felix, says, 'The bright altars are crowned with thronging lamps. Lights are burnt fragrant with waxed papyri. Day and night they burn; thus night is radiant with the brightness of day, and the day itself, bright in heavenly beauty, shines still more, its light doubled by countless lanterns.'[2]

The Roman screen was very similar in style to the earlier Byzantine screens. (See Plate 13(*a*).) Such a screen is best described by the term *regula*. An early example is to be seen in the catacombs of Januarius[3] at Naples; but other examples may be seen at Santa Maria in Cosmedin, Rome, and in other parts of Italy such as Torcello Cathedral, and at Grado, Santa Maria delle Grazie.[4] In some instances, such as San Clemente, Rome, and Sant' Apollinare Nuovo, Ravenna, only the lower portion or wainscotting of the screen appears to have been erected. Both in East and West it should be noted these screens were immediately in front of the altar and did not enclose the choir as in the case of the English medieval rood screen. The modern iconostasis in the Eastern rites occupies the same proximity to the altar, and thereby the altar is closer to the nave than in the medieval chancel.

In North Africa the altar sometimes stood further away from the apse than was the case in Italy, thus bringing it down into the nave two or three bays. In which case there was not only a screen or *regula*

---

[1] D.A.C.L., Tome 7, 32–5.
[2] *Nat. S. Fel.*, XIV, 99 in C.S.E.L., Tome XXX, p. 49.
[3] D.A.C.L., Tome 7, 31.
[4] F. van der Meer and C. Mohrmann, *Atlas of the Early Christian World*, 276 (1958).

on the side of the altar facing the congregation, but also there were screens enclosing the ends of the altar facing the north and south arcades of the nave, as we can see at El Asaba, Tripolitania,[1] and at Theveste, Algeria.[2]

For a reasoned perspective of the development of the screen before the altar in Eastern Christendom we express our indebtedness to several Eastern ecclesiologists, whose writings are comparatively unknown in the West.[3]

The term *iconostasis* (εἰκονόστασις) appears first in the sixth-century writer, Codinus,[4] where it means a picture-stand, a pedestal for holding a painting. It was customary for the Byzantine Emperors to set up such a stand in one of the apartments of the palace, on Christmas Eve, on which were hung pictures of Christ and other paintings. At first portable icons or pictures were sometimes hung on the pillars of the altar screen, as well as on the piers and walls of the nave. It should be remembered that in a Byzantine church, the altar screen was destined originally to serve a constructive purpose, and that it also offered an opportunity for the introduction of decorative sculpture and chisel work, to which the Byzantines were particularly partial. (See Plate 13(*b*).) The portable icons hung on the pillars of the screen were few in number and small in size, being made of mosaics and enamels. They were hung about the height of a man's head. We notice, too, that the old Byzantine screens were of marble or stone whereas the modern iconostasis tends usually to be made of wood. Even as late as the fourteenth century, the churches of Mistra in the Peloponnesus near Sparta show traces of sculpture and architectural motives on the screens which prove that Byzantium could not have been the original source of the solid wooden screen covered with paintings.[5]

It is to Russia and in the region of Novgorod, at the end of the fourteenth and the beginning of the fifteenth centuries, in the time of the celebrated Russian icon painter, Andrew Roublieu, that we must look for the present form of the Eastern iconostasis.[6] The vast dominions which Novgorod had colonized from the Baltic to the Urals, thrust

[1] *Archaeologia*, Vol. 95, pp. 34–5 (1953).
[2] J. N. Comper: op. cit., p. 68.
[3] S. D. Filimonoff: *The Church of St. Nicholas of Lipna, the problem of the original form of the iconostasis in Russian Churches* (Moscow, 1896) (in Russian); also P. Mouratoff: *L'ancienne peinture russe*, pp. 100–7 (Prague and Rome, 1925); also S. Salaville: *Introduction to the Study of Eastern Liturgies*, ed. J. M. T. Barton, pp. 105–12 (1938). See also *Echos d'Orient*, T. 28, pp. 454–8 (Paris, 1929).
[4] *De officiis aulae byzantinae*, c. VI (P.G., Tome 157, 61).
[5] Salaville: op. cit., p. 109. See also, O. M. Dalton: *Byzantine Art and Archaeology* (1911), pp. 164–5.
[6] H. Brockhaus: *Die Kunst in den Athos-Klöstern*, p. 18 (Leipszig, 1891).

back upon the commercial metropolis the customs of sylvan, well-wooded Russia. Sooner or later, these autochthonous tendencies were to triumph over the traditions imported from Byzantium, the city of marble. In the history of Russian painting the triumph is that of icon-painting over fresco.[1]

In the history of architecture, it is the triumph of the immense wooden screen, covered entirely with paintings, over the Byzantine *templon*, made of stone or marble, with its small portable mosaic pictures. No doubt the iconoclastic controversy had some bearing on the development of the painted icon instead of sculpture. Another cause was the abundance of these icons, which accumulated in churches and led to the formation of rows of superimposed ranks of icons. (See Plate 21.)

In the Syrian and Coptic rites screens made of stone or of lattice-work are the usual custom; but there are no pictures or icons on them. This undoubtedly reflects the older customs of Eastern Christendom.[2]

(b) *Behind the altar*

We shall be giving reasons for the placing of the altar close to the eastern wall or apse in some of the Syrian churches. (See p. 91.) Nevertheless, it is probably true to state that during the earlier centuries it was the more general custom for the altar to be free-standing. This continues to be the custom in the Eastern Orthodox rite; but the celebrant does not face the people since churches in the Eastern rites are always orientated.

In the Roman basilica the altar normally stood on the chord of the apse at the western end of the church. While in North Africa, as at Theveste, it sometimes stood under its ciborium, two or three bays away from the apse. There is reason to believe that Anglo-Saxon churches had free-standing altars, although the celebrant did not face the people. The apse behind such altars was frequently decorated with frescoes or mosaics as we can still see in some of the older churches in Rome and Ravenna. (See Plate 1.)

The Carolingian era in the ninth century was a time of great activity and renaissance in the life of Western Christendom; and many innovations were introduced which, although in an incipient form at

[1] Mouratoff: op. cit., p. 105.
[2] H. W. Codrington: *Studies of the Syrian Liturgies*, p. 3 (1952); also A. A. King, *The Rites of Eastern Christendom* (1947), Vol. I, p. 379.

that time, were to have far-reaching effects in matters affecting the administration of the sacraments. The writings of Alcuin (d. 804), Amalarius of Metz (d. *circa* 850) and Rhabanus Maurus (d. 856), all contain references to ceremonial changes of that era. It is, however, to a Synodical Admonition, attributed to Pope Leo IV (847–55), but probably of Gallican origin and incorporated into many tenth-century documents, that we turn for an innovation that was to have considerable effect in the structure and development of the altar and which reads: 'Let nothing be placed upon the altar except the chests and relics, or perhaps the four gospels and a pyx, with the body of the Lord for the viaticum of the sick.'[1]

Hitherto, the placing of anything on the altar apart from the vessels for the Eucharist and the Book of the Gospels had been discouraged and forbidden. Thus in the earlier period, neither cross nor candlesticks stood on the altar. The innovation of placing chests with relics on the mensa was an invasion of a principle which, until then, had been carefully observed.

Relics were of three kinds: (1) The body of a saint, or a portion of that body; (2) clothes worn by him; and (3) pieces of cloth brought into contact with his tomb. To which may be added relics of fragments of the reputed True Cross. Relics of the True Cross and portions of the body of a saint were kept in small caskets, which came to be stood on the altar during the Mass. Sometimes they were incorporated into a small portable triptych, which stood on the back of the altar. (See Plate 14.)

In the West, in the earlier period, the complete bodies of saints were buried under the altar, there being an aversion to the dismemberment of the body. But from the sixth century the dismemberment of the bodies of saints increased; and these portions came to be incorporated or carried in portable reliquaries or shrines of various forms. (See Plate 15.)

But in great churches, where there was the body of a famous saint, the retention of a coffin or reliquary containing the complete body was regarded as essential, particularly as this brought large numbers of pilgrims to the church. As these pilgrimages increased there came a demand for greater prominence being given to the display of the reliquary or shrine, which hitherto had lain under the altar. How was this combination of altar and raised shrine to be carried out? The reliquary was placed at right angles to the altar, close to the back;

[1] P.L., Tome 132, 456.

or else it rested on a low retable for the sake of giving to the whole height and dignity. Thus one end of the shrine rested on the back of the altar, while the other end was supported by stone piers or masonry. At the time the altar was still of the shape of a cube, and therefore the end of the shrine acted as a kind of reredos to the altar.

This arrangement, whereby the end of the reliquary or shrine formed a reredos at the back of the altar seems to have prevailed at old St. Paul's with the shrine of St. Erkenwald in the early fourteenth century, and at Chichester with St. Richard's shrine.[1] Also Matthew Paris (d. 1259) in his *Vitae S. Albani Abbatum* tells us of a similar arrangement at St. Albans, whereby the end of the shrine rested on the back of the altar during the time of Abbot Simon.[2] This, of course, was before the erection of the great screen separating the High altar from the shrine in the fifteenth century.

But this combination of altar and shrine meant the ciborium could only be retained with difficulty; and it came to be transferred from a position immediately over the altar to one over the shrine (see Plate 16) as at Lorsch, where, in the late tenth century, it is described as *super requiem martyris*.[3]

The final separation of the altar from its shrine or feretory took place at the end of the fourteenth and the beginning of the fifteenth century, when a stone screen was erected behind the High altar of a number of the greater churches, while the shrine was placed east of the screen. Thereby the pilgrims were able to pray at the shrine without interrupting the services held in the choir and at the altar. Examples of such screens may be seen at Westminster Abbey,[4] St. Albans Cathedral, and Christchurch Priory. In the case of the Westminster screen, it is only one stage in height; but the others soar up to the clerestory.

These English screens behind the altar differ considerably from the vast baroque altar-pieces that can be seen in a number of Spanish cathedrals, such as Burgos, and the Italian examples, such as that in the Church of the Gesù at Rome. In these later Spanish and Italian examples the altar has become a mere pediment below a glorified and flamboyant east wall. (See Plate 17.) Immediately behind and above

---

[1] F. Bond: *Introduction to English Church Architecture*, Vol. 1, p. 91 (1913).

[2] Rolls Series, Vol. 28.1.189. Et loco suo eminentiori, scilicet, supra majus altare, contra frontem celebrantis collocavit, ut facie et corde habeat quilibet celebrans missam super idem altare martyris memoriam. Et idcirco in objecto visus celebrantis, martyrium eiusdem, scilicet decollatio, figuratur.

[3] E. Bishop: *Liturgica Historica*, p. 27.

[4] J. Perkins: *Westminster Abbey*, Vol. 1, pp. 42–4.

the English altar screen, as we can still see at St. Albans, Winchester and Southwark Cathedrals, is a framed rectangle about four feet in height and corresponding in length to that of the altar. This is the reredos-proper, and it contained sculpture on a smaller scale and proportions to that on the higher stages of the screen; or sometimes the rectangle was filled with an embroidered cloth known as the 'super-frontal,' usually corresponding with the nether frontal that covered the altar itself during the late middle ages.

In Germany and the Low Countries, another kind of altar-piece is found in the late medieval period, usually made of wood, sometimes containing carved figures in niches, and in other instances having painted figures in panels. This type of screen, known as a triptych, had two leaves which could be closed over the middle member during Lent. Some of these triptychs tended to dominate the altar, as we can see by the many examples provided by Father Braun in his monumental study. (See also Plate 20.)

The reredos in the English parish church of the late medieval period never reached the same proportions or dominance that it did in some other countries of Western Europe. The square east end and the large and low east window, or series of lancets, tended to keep the reredos from attaining undue prominence in England. In some instances, such as Salle, Norfolk, the sill of the east window came down to the level of the mensa. But in very many instances there is a space on the wall between the sill of the east window and the top of the altar between three and four feet. This was sometimes filled in with a stone or alabaster reredos with figures sculptured in niches. While in other cases there was a painted reredos or else a fabric hanging known as the dorsal or super-frontal. But whichever form of reredos or dorsal was adopted, this retable or altar-piece in the English parish church was long and low. (See Plate 18.)

While it is true to state in general terms that the High altar during the first millennium was usually free-standing, evidence for reredoses in connexion with lesser or side altars antedates by several centuries that for High altars. From the eighth and ninth centuries the multiplication of side altars begins,[1] and there are many instances where such altars stood close to a wall or pier.

Indeed, the Eucharist which was celebrated in the catacombs on the anniversary of a martyr's death took place over his tomb,

---

[1] Braun: op. cit., Vol. 1, pp. 372 and 389.

which was sometimes in a recess or *arcosolium* which had a fresco painted in the background.[1] What was this but a form of reredos?

The fifth century altar in the baptistry at St. John Lateran seems to have stood against a recessed wall.[2] Behind an altar in the crypt of Urbano alla Caffarella is a painted reredos of the eighth century. In the Chapel of St. Zeno in St. Prassede, Rome, is a painted niche and altar of the ninth century.[3] An early ninth century altar complete with ciborium stands against the east wall of the north aisle of Sant' Apollinare in Classe, Ravenna; and it has a carved reredos of the same period.[4] (See Plate 3.)

In the post-Reformation era, in Southern Europe, the towering *retabulo* developed in Spain and Italy, but it never reached the same proportions in France, where a greater sense of the purpose of the altar prevailed during the seventeenth and eighteenth centuries. In England the altar-pieces, which are a feature of the churches erected by Wren, Hawksmoor and Gibbs, often have an east window above them. These reredoses frequently had two panels on which were inscribed the Lord's Prayer, the Ten Commandments and the Apostles' Creed. (See Plate 10.) Thus English baroque differs considerably from its Italian and Spanish counterparts. (See Plate 17.)

[1] D.A.C.L., Tome 1, 3162.
[2] Ibid., Tome 2, 419–20.
[3] F. Bond: *The Chancels of English Parish Churches*, p. 52 (1916).
[4] G. Bovini: *The Churches of Ravenna*, p. 163 (Novara, Italy, 1960).

5

Orientation at Prayer and the Position of the Celebrant at the Altar

In spite of the refusal of confessors and martyrs to offer incense before the statue of the Emperor, it is unlikely that primitive Christianity was entirely unaffected by the culture and civilization in which it grew up. We must, therefore, seek not only in Judaism but also to some degree in the Graeco-Roman world for the origins of some of the forms of Christian worship. Some of the adaptations from the pagan sphere were made at a time when paganism no longer held sway; or else they involved cases where the ceremonial was capable of a Christian interpretation.

Amongst such customs must be considered that of praying to the east during prayer. This custom appears to have been known, in some degree both to Jews and pagans alike. To pray towards the east was a fixed custom not only among the Romans and Greeks, but also with many other peoples. (See *Ezek*. viii. 16.)

The east, where the sun rises, appeared to men as the region from whence proceeded life, power and happiness. The rising sun became the symbol of divinity; and, in fact, the sun itself became deified. But orientation itself remained independent of such false notions and thus became adopted into Christian worship.[1]

The Jews had some conception of orientation at prayer. Thus 'and when Daniel knew the writing was signed, he went into his house (now his windows were open towards Jerusalem), and he kneeled upon his knees three times a day, and prayed' (*Dan*. vi. 10). The Mishna also commanded Jews to follow this practice and only under exceptional circumstances were relaxations permitted: 'Whoever is riding on a donkey descends for his prayer, and if he is not able to alight, so let him turn his heart to the house of the All-Holy.'[2]

[1] F. Doelger: *Sol Salutis*, Münster (1925), p. 210.
[2] J. A. Jungmann: *The Early Liturgy* (1960), p. 135.

Also in later times the east came to be associated in Jewish devotion with the region from whence the Messiah would come; and in the Vulgate and Septuagint texts of Psalm lxviii. 33, we have: 'Sing to God that rideth on the heaven of heavens, eastward: lo, he will utter a mighty sound with his words.' So also the writer of the Book of Baruch says: 'O Jerusalem, look about thee toward the east, and behold the joy that cometh unto thee from God' (*Baruch* iv. 36). This passage was used later by the Christian Church on Palm Sunday for our Lord's entry into Jerusalem.

The oldest Palestinian synagogues were 'orientated' so that the worshippers faced Jerusalem. Thus in general archaeological research has shown that in Galilee the buildings faced south, those in trans-Jordan faced west, and western synagogues faced towards the east.[1]

From Elchasai, the founder of a Judaeo-Christian sect, we learn that he told his adherents to pray towards Jerusalem and not towards the east. According to Jungmann,[2] this indicates that as early as the first century Christians were praying towards the east. Finally, we have the Song of Zechariah, 'Because of the tender mercy of our God; whereby the day-spring (literally, 'orient-light') shall visit us' (*Luke* i. 78).

The Ascension of Christ was believed to have taken place on the Mount of Olives to the east of Jerusalem. So also his second Advent would be from the east. In the primitive Church the Parousia and the second Advent were very vivid in the minds of the worshippers; and turning to the east meant turning to the glorified Christ who would come from the orient since he had gone up in the east. The Shepherd of Hermas sees the Ecclesia or personification of the Church coming down to earth from the east: 'While she yet spake with me, certain two men appeared, and lifted up their arms, and went away towards the east, where also the chair was.'[3]

In the third century the Emperor Aurelian brought to Rome from the Orient the cult of the *Sol invictus*. In reply to this, Christians began to emphasize the fact that Christ is their Sun. 'Who is so invincible as our Lord who conquered death?' asks a Christmas sermon of that period.[4] In the fourth century the feast of the *Sol invictus* on December 25th was replaced at Rome by the feast of the Nativity of Christ, which hitherto had been observed on January 6th. Thereby an attempt

[1] A. C. Bouquet: *Everyday Life in the New Testamant* (1953), p. 210.
[2] *The Early Liturgy*, p. 135.
[3] *Hermas*, 1.4, 3.
[4] Doelger: op. cit., p. 291.

was made to Christianize a pagan cult connected with the sun. But as late as A.D. 450 Pope Leo the Great observed in a sermon that some Christians having climbed the steps of St. Peter's, Rome, turned round and bowed toward the rising sun.[1]

Both in private and liturgical prayer there is considerable evidence that Christians faced toward the east from the earliest times. In the second century in Syria the room where prayer was normally made had a cross on the east wall, and to which the worshippers turned.[2] This was not unconnected with the idea of the Second Advent, to which we have already alluded. It was believed that the return of Christ would be heralded in the east by the sign of the Cross in the heavens.[3] This belief was based on the words of Christ: 'Then shall appear the sign of the Son of Man in heaven' (*Matt.* xxiv. 30). It is almost certain that the writer of the *Didache* (*circa* A.D. 100) in his sixteenth chapter has the same phenomenon in mind when he says 'Then shall appear the signs of truth. First the sign spread out in heaven, then the sign of the sound of the trumpet, and thirdly the resurrection of the dead.'[4]

In the North African Church we find the same ideas of prayer towards the orient. Thus Tertullian (d. A.D. 230) tells us in the sixteenth chapter of his *Apology*: 'We shall be counted Persians, perhaps, though we do not worship the orb of day painted on a piece of linen cloth, having himself everywhere in his own disk. The idea no doubt has originated from our being known to turn to the east in prayer.'[5] In his treatise against the Valentinians, Chapter 3, he says: 'Of our dove, however, how simple is the very house, always in high and open places and facing the light. As the symbol of the Holy Spirit, it loves the east, that figure of Christ.' There is also the greatest of the North African Fathers, St. Augustine, who tells us in *De Sermone Domini in Monte*, Bk. 2, chapter 5, 'And for the purpose of showing this, when we stand at prayer, we turn to the east, whence the heaven rises.'[6]

We do not possess many details as to the liturgical and ceremonial arrangements of house-churches and other buildings used for Christian worship in the pre-Nicene era. But the information which is available suggests that the orientation of both celebrant and people was not unknown. Thus in the house-church at Dura-Europos in Mesopotamia,

---

[1] P.L., Tome 54, 218.
[2] E. Peterson: 'La Croce e La Preghiera verso oriente' in *Ephemerides Liturgicae*, LIX, pp. 52–3, Rome, 1945.
[3] Ibid., p. 64; also E. Syndicus: *Early Christian Art* (1962), p. 103.
[4] K. Lake: op. cit., pp. 332–3.   [5] P.L., Tome 1, 570.   [6] Ibid., Tome 34, 1277.

which is dated about A.D. 232, the room used for the Eucharistic celebration appears to have had a *bema* or platform at its eastern end upon which the Holy Table stood.[1]

The writer of the *Didascalia*, about the same date, says: 'Let the lay men sit in another part of the house towards the east. For it so should be, that in the eastern part of the house, the presbyters sit with the bishops, and next the lay men, and then the women also. For it is required that you pray toward the east, as knowing that which is written: *Give ye glory to God, who rideth upon the heaven of heavens towards the east.*'[2]

More important, however, than the foregoing examples is the house-church at Qirk-Bizzé in North Syria, which is the exemplar of an important liturgical arrangement, of which a number of other examples are now known to us in Syria. The building was usually orientated. Midway down the nave of the church there was an inverted horse-shoe-like chancel, which had no opening in the middle. Inside the 'horse-shoe' screen there was a stone bench with the bishop's seat in the middle. For the first part of the liturgy, the bishop and his assistants sat or stood inside this chancel with their backs to the congregation, thus occupying an inverted position from that in the Roman basilica. In front of the bishop and his ministers, and surmounted by a canopy or ciborium there stood a small altar-like table from which the prayers and lections were conducted during the first part of the liturgy. At the time of the offertory the bishop and his assistants advanced to the altar proper, which stood close to the east wall or apse, and with their backs to the congregation took the eastward position for the Eucharistic Prayer.[3] (See Plate 19.)

Therefore the assumption widely stated in recent years that during the early centuries the celebrant invariably stood on the other side of the altar facing the people can no longer be maintained. Also it has been asserted more than once that the axis or alignment of the early Roman basilicas was so varied that they were constructed with no regard to the principle of orientation, and that at Rome during the first six centuries, as in modern times, orientation was disregarded. On the face of it, this view may seem plausible enough; but the scholar and student will treat with caution any theory which appears to be based on certain *a priori* assumptions and presuppositions which are

[1] D.A.C.L., Tome 15, 1863–4; also J. W. Crowfoot: *Early Churches of Palestine*, p. 3 (1941).
[2] R. H. Connolly: *Didascalia Apostolorum*, pp. 119–20 (1929).
[3] Cf. D.A.C.L., Tome 15, 1866–80; see also H. W. Codrington, op. cit., pp. 62–4.

held in order to further a particular form of the celebration of the
Eucharist in our own times. We have already shown that in the case
of the Syrian liturgical arrangement the celebrant stood facing east
with his back to the people, and therefore the custom of celebrating
Mass *versus populum* was not the invariable custom of the first centuries
of Christian worship. Liturgical reformers anxious to promote this
custom have been misled into supposing that orientation of the celebrant was not observed in the so-called Basilican rite. But in so doing
they have ignored the detailed study and survey which the late George
Gilbert Scott gave to the orientation of over forty basilicas in and
around the city of Rome.[1] In no case does any basilica face due north
or due south; which would certainly have been the case in some instances, in so great a number of churches, had orientation been completely disregarded. In most cases Scott shows that the altar stands at
the western end or apse. So that when the celebrant stood on the far
side of the altar he faced east, and incidentally the people. The varia-
tions from due west in these basilicas are no greater than those which
are accepted in an orientated church, where 'east' is understood to
mean any point between north-east and south-east. Thus St. Peter's
(Vatican) faces west, St. John Lateran west, St. Mary Major north-
west. The notable exception appears to be St. Paul's outside-the-
walls, which has its altar at the east end; but evidence exists that this
church as built by Constantine the Great faced west.[2] St. Laurence
outside-the-walls had its altar at the west end until 1216, when the
axis of the church was completely reversed by Pope Honorius III.[3]

Another cause for the celebrant having to stand facing the people
in the Roman basilican rite was the fact that the altar was frequently
built over the tomb or reliquary of the martyr or saint to whom the
church was dedicated. This arrangement is usually known as the
'confessio.'[4] Often there was an opening or grille on the nave-side of
the *confessio* under the altar. Through this opening it was customary
for people to insert cloths and other objects which were believed to gain
a therapeutic or healing value if they came into contact with the saint's
coffin or reliquary. This *fenestella* or opening in the *confessio* meant
there could be no *predella* or foot-pace on the nave side of the altar
upon which the celebrant could stand; hence he had to stand on the
far side *versus populum*.[5] But where no *confessio* with its opening existed

---

[1] G. G. Scott, Junior: *An Essay on the History of English Church Architecture*, pp. 17–23. (1881).
[2] J. W. Franklin: *The Cathedrals of Italy*, p. 102 (1957).
[3] Scott: op. cit., p. 18; also D.A.C.L., Tome 8, 1943. See also Appendix, p. 108.
[4] D.A.C.L., Tome 3, 2503–8; also J. G. Davies: *Early Christian Church Architecture*, pp. 85–6 (1952).
[5] J. Braun: *Der christliche Altar*, Vol. 1, p. 412; also J. A. Jungmann: *The Mass of the Roman Rite*, Vol. 1, p. 255.

it does not seem to be the case in the basilican rite that the celebrant faced the people. Thus in the basilica of Castel Sant' Elia near Nepi in Central Italy, there is an ancient altar complete with its ciborium; but there is no *confessio*, and consequently the foot-pace is on the nave side of the altar, and the celebrant stands with his back to the people. (See Plate 1.) In some instances, as at St. Laurence's, Rome, there was a staircase by which access was gained to the reliquary; and the opening for the staircase was on the nave side of the altar thus preventing the celebrant from standing on that side.

The late Dr. W. H. Frere[1] and other liturgical scholars were perplexed by the apparent contradiction in the text of *Ordo Romanus Primus*, which said the pontiff turned round for the *Gloria in Excelsis* and the Collect of the day. This *Ordo*, in its original text, describes the papal Mass in St. Mary Major on Easter Day in the seventh century. This would have meant, according to Mabillon's uncritical text, which was the only text then available to Dr. Frere, that at the *Gloria in Excelsis* and the Collect of the day, the Pope, standing on the other side of the altar facing the people, turned and recited the Collect facing the western apse behind the altar. But since 1948 Dr. M. Andrieu has shown that the original text at this point reads as follows: 'When they have finished (the kyries) let the pontiff begin the *Gloria in Excelsis*, if it is the season, and he does not sit before they say Amen to the Collect which follows.'[2]

When this *Ordo* passed in the ninth century to be used in Gaul in a church where the celebrant stood with his back to the congregation in an orientated building, this section of the text was amended, as Andrieu has demonstrated, to read as follows: 'When they have finished, the pontiff turns himself round to the people, and begins the *Gloria in Excelsis*, and at once turns back again to the east until it is finished. Then after turning to the people again, he says *Peace be with you*, and turns himself again to the east saying, *Let us pray*, and the Collect follows.'[3] Thus Andrieu's critical study of this *Ordo* shows that the position of the celebrant was governed by the occidentation or orientation of the building in which the liturgy was celebrated.

The statement made by the late Edmund Bishop,[4] and copied by a number of commentators, that the introduction of a reliquary chest on the back of the altar in the ninth century was the cause of the

---

[1] W. H. Frere: *The Principles of Religious Ceremonial*, pp. 62 and 208 (new ed. 1928).
[2] M. Andrieu: *Les Ordines Romani*, p. 84, Vol. 2 (1948).
[3] Ibid., pp. 55, 84 and 144.
[4] E. Bishop: *Liturgica Historica*, pp. 27–8 (1918).

celebrant abandoning Mass *versus populum*, and coming to stand with his back to the people will no longer bear serious investigation, since it ignores important evidence from Anglo-Saxon and other sources:

(i) The *Sacramentary of Drogon* (Bibliothèque Nat., Paris, MS. 9428), belonging to the ninth century, has several illustrations both on the carved ivory cover, and in the manuscript pages, which show the celebrant taking the eastward position at an altar which has no reredos or reliquary on it, and is under a ciborium.[1]

(ii) The *Anglo-Saxon Psalter* (Brit. Mus. MS. Harl. 603, fol. 29v) has an illustration of a bishop standing on the near side of an altar which has only a paten and chalice on it and is under a ciborium. There is neither reredos, nor reliquary.

(iii) The late tenth century *Benedictional of Ethelwold* (Brit. Mus. MS. 49598 Fol. 118v) has an illustration of a bishop standing on the near side of an altar from which he has turned to bless the people. This altar has only a chalice and paten on it and stands under a ciborium.[2] (See Frontispiece.)

(iv) More important than this pictorial evidence, however, is the evidence for the position of the celebrant at Mass in Canterbury Cathedral, prior to the fire of A.D. 1067, when the larger part of the church was rebuilt. There was an altar at the east end of the monk's choir at which the celebrant stood with his back to the choir taking the eastward position. But there was also a western apse, where the celebrant stood on the further side of the altar facing east and the congregation. Eadmer (d. *circa* 1124), the precentor of Canterbury, and the friend of St. Anselm, remembered these liturgical arrangements prior to the rebuilding after the fire of 1067. He was a boy at Canterbury; and he leaves no doubt that the celebrant stood on the other side of the altar in the western apse in order to face east.[3]

(v) The simple and somewhat humble structures in the form of Celtic oratories, which are still in evidence in the remoter parts of the British Isles, notably in Scotland and Ireland,[4] are almost always orientated. The entrance is at the west end and there is an opening or window at the east end, which is invariably square-ended and not

[1] De Fleury: *La Messe*, Vol. 1, pp. 66-7, and Plates 4 and 5 (Paris, 1883); also D.A.C.L., Tome 4, 1540–2.
[2] See also F. Wormald: *The Benedictional of St. Ethelwold* (1959), p. 30.
[3] Rolls Series, Vol. 73, i.9. Ad hoc altare cum sacerdos ageret divina mysteria, faciem ad populum qui deorsum stabat ad orientem, versum habeat.
[4] D.A.C.L., Tome 2, 2920–30. H. G. Leask: *Irish Churches* (1955), Vol. I, pp. 5–78.

apsidal; and near this window stood the altar. While most of the oratories that are now standing are not earlier than the seventh and eighth centuries, there is the interesting evidence and testimony in Celtic Latin that St. Patrick (d. 466) celebrated facing east.[1]

It is certainly the case in Italy from the baroque era that the occidentation or orientation of church buildings has been ignored; but it is incorrect to imply that this was the case in earlier times. Outside the city of Rome the basilican arrangement prevailed in some places. Thus at Terracina Cathedral in the Province of Latium the portals of the building are facing east and consequently the altar is at the western end. The celebrant stands on the far side of the altar facing east when he celebrates Mass. This arrangement prevails not only at the high altar, but at the side altars which stand at the western ends of the north and south aisles. This is no modern liturgical reform, since all three altars are ancient and each has its *confessio* with an opening on the nave side. (See Plate 28.)

In North Africa a number of churches are known to have been occidentated; but here again there appears to have been a special reason for this since the altar was built over a *confessio*. This was the case at Theveste,[2] Thabacra,[3] El Asaba[4] and at Carthage, where the bodies of St. Perpetua and her companions were buried in the *confessio* of the *basilica majorum*.[5]

It is sometimes suggested that the presence of the bishop's throne in the eastern apse of Norwich Cathedral is evidence for the custom of celebrating *versus populum*, but no conclusive evidence has been submitted to uphold this contention; and it is not supported by any evidence in the medieval service books still extant and belonging to that cathedral.[6]

There is the parallel case of the bishop's throne in the cathedral church of Lyons, France, where the Archbishop sits or stands during the first part of the liturgy, but he comes round and takes the eastward position at the altar for the consecration of the Eucharist.[7] This seems to have been the custom at Norwich. It is also the custom in the Eastern Orthodox rite.

[1] Ibid., col. 2995. Incantabit nefas a sua mensa ex anteriore parte domus suae.
[2] J. N. Comper: *Further Thoughts on the English Altar*, pp. 69–70 (1932); also D.A.C.L., Tome 15, 2006–9.
[3] D.A.C.L., Tome 4, 2231–2; also Tome 15, 2146–52.
[4] *Archaeologia*, Vol. 95, pp. 34–5 (1953).
[5] D.A.C.L., Tome 14, 432; also Tome 10, 2234–8.
[6] Cf. J. B. L. Tolhurst: *The Customary of the Cathedral Priory Church of Norwich*, 1948 (H.B.S., Vol. 82).
[7] D. Buenner: *L'Ancienne Liturgie Romaine — Le Rite Lyonnais* (Lyons, 1934), pp. 332–4.

The Abbey Churches of St. Gall and Fulda in the ninth century appear to have had a similar arrangement to that at Canterbury whereby there was an altar at the eastern and western ends of the church.[1]

Durandus, Bishop of Mende (d. 1296), in his celebrated work on religious symbolism recognizes that the celebrant may stand on either side of the altar, but this position is governed by the orientation or occidentation of the church building: 'The priest at the altar and in the divine office ought, according to the constitution of Vigilius, Pope (d. 555), always to pray towards the east; whence in churches which have the doors at the west, he that celebrates turns in the salutations to the people; but in churches which have the entrance at the east, as at Rome, there is no need in the salutations for turning round, because the priest always turns to the people.'[2]

In Germany and France as well as in Britain churches were usually built with the altar at the east end. But the reversed orientation of Mainz Cathedral, built by Archbishop Willigis in 978, probably reflects the influence of old St. Peter's, Rome;[3] since at that time the Emperors Otto I and II with their court and ecclesiastical entourage made several visits to Rome. This 'romanizing' influence is reflected not only in the planning and ceremonial arrangements at Mainz, but also in the Romano-Germanic Pontifical which was compiled at Mainz in the same period.[4] A tenth-century ivory diptych of Ottonian craftsmanship,[5] one panel of which is in the Fitzwilliam Museum, Cambridge, and the other in the State Library at Frankfort, seems to depict the reversed orientation of Mainz Cathedral at that period. It shows an archbishop celebrating the pontifical liturgy *versus populum*. This arrangement in a church north of the Alps would have been unusual at that time; and it can only have been due to the occidentation of Archbishop Willigis's cathedral to which we have alluded.

Thus there is continuous evidence from the primitive era until the late middle ages that the position of the celebrant at the altar was generally governed by the orientation or occidentation of the church

---

[1] J. Braun: *Der christliche Altar*, Vol. 1, p. 389.
[2] G. Durandus: *Rationale Divinorum Officiorum*, ed. J. Beletho, Lib. 5.1, 57 (p. 340) (Naples, 1859). Sacerdos in altari et in divinis officiis debet ex institutione Vigilii Papae versus orientem orare. Unde in ecclesiis ostium ad occidente habentibus missam celebrans in salutatione ad populum se vertit, quia quos salutamus, facie ad faciem praesentamus et deinde oraturus se ad orientem convertit. In ecclesiis vero, ostia ad orientem habentibus, ut Romae, nulla est in salutatione necessaria conversio. Sacerdos in illis celebrans semper stat ad populum conversus.
[3] K. J. Conant: *Carolingian and Romanesque Architecture* (1959), p. 68.
[4] M. Andrieu: *Les Ordinex Romani*, Vol. 1, pp. 505–6, 512–3.
[5] Cf. Albert Boeckler: *Elfenbeinreliefs der Ottonischen Renaissance* in *Phoebus* II (Basle, 1949), p. 144.

PLATE 33

A MODERN ORTHODOX ALTAR

The sanctuary and altar of the Metropolitan Cathedral at Athens shows that the altar is free-standing, but is fully vested.

The throne and seats for the Archbishop and his assistants are behind the altar; but at the time of the Eucharistic Prayer the celebrant stands facing east with his back to the congregation in accordance with Byzantine tradition.

PLATE 34

A THROW-OVER FRONTAL

The altar in the American war memorial chapel of St. Paul's Cathedral designed by Mr. S. E. Dykes Bower and Mr. W. G. Allen.

The frontal envelopes the whole altar and is made of crimson silk velvet. There is an embroidered motif in gold and silver thread of a dove set in a golden sun.

buildings; and only in peculiar circumstances due to the difficulties of the site was there a departure from this custom which has been observed from high antiquity both in Eastern and Western Christendom.

The present Roman Missal recognizes that the celebrant may stand on either side of the altar; but the rubric which refers to this arrangement shows that the posture of the celebrant is governed by the axis or alignment of the church, 'Si altare sit ad orientem versus populum, non vertit humeros ad altare, cum dicturus est *Dominus vobiscum, Orate fratres, Ite Missa est,* vel daturus benedictionem.'[1]

There is no evidence during the first six centuries that the celebrant stood on the further side of the altar, and in so doing deliberately faced west, as is now the custom amongst certain Anglican liturgical reformers. To have done so, in the early period, would have contradicted all the emphasis on the east as the region of light and the west as the region of Satan and darkness. St. Cyril of Jerusalem,[2] St. Ambrose[3] and St. Jerome[4] all writing in the fourth century tell us that the candidates for baptism first turned west as the region of the devil and darkness and made their renunciations before turning east to God the true light.

Finally, in view of the oft-repeated statement that the celebrant facing the people is a factor today in bringing about a closer union between celebrant and congregation, it may be well to make clear that the historical precedent for this arrangement has been greatly exaggerated. The rites of Eastern Christendom have never countenanced this custom, although the altar has no reredos and is free-standing in the Eastern Orthodox rite. While the bishop's *synthronos* is in the apse, he comes and takes the eastward position and does not face the people, as all churches are orientated. This is worthy of note, since these rites generally have preserved the primitive and traditional practices of the Church more faithfully than has usually been the case in the West; while they have retained to this day an active participation of the congregation in the liturgy.[5]

---

[1] *Missale Romanum*, Ritus celebrandi missam, V.3, Auctoriate recognitum Romae, 1911, p. XLV.
[2] *St. Cyril of Jerusalem's Lectures on the Christian Sacraments* (Ed. F. L. Cross), pp. 13–6 and 54–8. (1951)
[3] Ambros. *de Initatis*, cap. 2. Ingressus ut adversarium tuum cerneres qui renunciandum mox putares, ad orientem converteris. Quia enim renunciat diabolo, ad Christum convertitur.
[4] Hieron., *in Amos* vi, 14. In mysteriis primum renunciamus ei qui in occidente est, nobisque moritur cum peccatis: et sic versi ad orientum, pactum inimus cum sole justitiae, et ei servitorus nos esse promittimus.
[5] J. A. Jungmann, *The Early Liturgy*, pp. 137–8.

G

It is the case that a number of ancient churches were planned architecturally on a central vertical axis. This has led in recent times to the assumption that the altar stood in the *middle* of the congregation in such buildings. This view is incorrect, and is not in accordance with established archaeological facts.

Circular buildings of pagan origin were sometimes adapted for Christian worship, such as the Pantheon at Rome. These did not have the altar in the middle of the church, nor were the centrally-planned buildings such as St. George's Ezra, San Vitale, Ravenna, the Holy Wisdom at Constantinople without an apsidal east end where the altar stood.[1]

The same must be said in regard to later churches having a central axis, such as the Palatinate Chapel of Charlemagne at Aachen (ninth century) and the round churches built by the Templars.[2] In all cases the altar stood in, or on the chord of, the apse and not in the middle of the congregation. In the case of the rotunda usually known as Santa Costanza, Rome, this building was originally built about A.D. 330 by Constantine the Great as a mausoleum to house the sarcophagus of his sister, Constantia. It was converted into a church by the placing of an altar in the centre during the pontificate of Alexander IV (1254–61). This altar has recently been removed; but it is not unlikely that some ecclesiologists have mistakenly assumed that the central altar was a feature of the original building.[3]

The expression *circumstantes* in the Roman Canon of the Mass has misled liturgical reformers in our own day into supposing that the congregation in the old Roman rite surrounded the altar on all sides; and consequently a plea is made for what is mistakenly supposed to be primitive practice in regard to a central altar. Dr. Joseph Jungmann, who is one of the most eminent exponents of the Roman liturgy, has replied to this argument as follows: 'During the first thousand years, standing was the principal posture during the canon. Note, however, that the *circum* is not to be construed as though the faithful had ever completely surrounded the altar. Rather the picture intended is what is suggested by the structure of the old Roman basilicas, where the altar stood between the presbytery and the nave, so that the faithful—especially if there was a transept—could form a semi-circle or "open-ring" around the altar.'[4]

[1] J. G. Davies: *Early Christian Church Architecture* (1952), pp. 51–80.
[2] K. J. Conant: *Carolingian and Romanesque Architecture* (1959), pp. 14–5.
[3] W. Macdonald: *Early Christian and Byzantine Architecture* (1962), p. 22–3.
[4] J. A. Jungmann: *The Mass of the Roman Rite*, Vol. 2, p. 166.

6

The Hanging Pyx

THE reader will find in our bibliography a number of works which deal with the general history of the reservation of the Blessed Sacrament. Our purpose here is to treat of one method of reserving the Eucharist about which there has been some controversy and confusion.

In the pre-Nicene period reservation was usually in private houses and on persons rather than in some place in the church building, and this arrangement seems to have prevailed until the sixth century, although conciliar legislation in the fourth and fifth centuries had tried to prevent it.[1] Indeed it would seem that not until the ninth century in the so-called *Statutes of Boniface* does legislation require the obligation of having the Sacrament reserved in the church.[2] Evidence at Rome, however, in the fifth and sixth centuries suggests that the Eucharist was reserved in a *turris* or tower.[3] Venantius Fortunatus (d. 609) wrote a poem on the golden eucharistic tower in use at Bourges.[4] The seventh-century Bobbio Missal mentions such a tower along with the chalice and paten.[5] In the seventh-century *Explanation of the Gallican Mass*, which is no longer ascribed to Germanus of Paris, it says: 'The Body of the Lord is carried in towers, because the tomb of the Lord was cut out of rock in the shape of a tower.'[6] But it is by no means certain that such towers were suspended above the altar, or indeed that they always contained the consecrated Elements. In some circumstances these towers are known to have been used for carrying the prepared bread at the offertory in the Gallican rite as Gregory of Tours testifies in the sixth century.[7] The first explicit reference to the custom of suspending a vessel with the reserved Sacrament over or above the altar is in a ninth-century document by the pseudo-Amphilochius under the title of *Vita Basilii*, in which it is related that the Saint caused a golden dove to be fashioned, and, having placed in it a portion of the Sacred Bread, hung it above the altar.[8]

[1] S. J. P. van Dijk and J. H. Walker: *The Myth of the Aumbry*, p. 25.
[2] Mansi, Tome 12, 383.
[3] Van Dijk and Walker: op. cit., p. 28.
[4] P.L., Tome 88, 144; also *Venanti Fortunati Carmina*, ed. F. Leo and B. Krusch in M.G.H. *Auct. Antiq.*, iv. (1881), p. 71.
[5] E. A. Lowe: *The Bobbio Missal*, p. 169 (H.B.S., Vol. 58 (1920)).
[6] P.L., Tome 72, 93.
[7] Ibid., Tome 71, 781.
[8] *In Vitam Basilii* in F. Combefis: *SS.PP. Amphilochii Iconensis etc.* (Paris, 1644), p. 176.

In England the earliest reference to the Sacrament hanging over the altar is in the twelfth-century *Chronicle* of Roger Hoveden, who tells us that on Candlemas Day, 1141, while King Stephen was at Mass at Lincoln the pyx above the altar which held the Lord's Body fell when the chain suddenly broke.[1]

From that time until the Reformation era there is abundant evidence that the hanging pyx was in use all over England, although Lyndwood, the English Canonist in the fifteenth century,[2] seems to have preferred the wall aumbry which he had seen in Portugal and Holland. At Salisbury Cathedral in 1220 there was 'a handsome *cuppa*, silver gilt within and without, for the reception of the Eucharist, with a silver hoop which was to be hung over the High altar.'[3] The Sarum Inventory known as the *Register of St. Osmund* covering the years 1214–1220, shows also that there was a silver dove in a hoop for the Eucharist.[4] But this example of a Eucharistic Dove in England for the reservation of the Blessed Sacrament appears to be exceptional as no other example is known here.

One of the fullest and best-known instances of the hanging pyx is recorded in the sixteenth-century *Rites of Durham*, the spelling of which we have modernized: 'Over the High Altar did hang a rich and most sumptuous canopy for the Blessed Sacrament to hang within it, which had two irons fastened in the French Peere,[5] very finely gilt, which held the canopy over the midst of the said High Altar (that the Pyx did hang in it, that it could not move nor stir), whereon did stand a Pelican, all of silver, upon the height of the said canopy, very finely gilded, giving her blood for the sins of the world; and it was goodly to behold, for the Blessed Sacrament to hang in, and a marvellous fair pyx that the Holy Blessed Sacrament did hang in, which was of the most pure fine gold, and most curiously wrought of goldsmith work. And the white cloth that hung over the pyx was of very fine lawn, all embroidered and wrought about with gold and red silk, and four great and round knops of gold, marvellously and cunningly wrought, with great tassels of gold and red silk hanging at them, and at the four corners of the white lawn cloth, and the crook that hung with the cloth

---

[1] Rog. Hoveden, *Chron.* (Rolls Soc. Vol. 51. i.201. Cecidit super altare pixis, cui Corpus Domini inerat, abrupto vinculo).

[2] *Provinciale*, III, 25 (Oxoniae, 1679).

[3] Rolls Soc. Vol. 78. ii.13.

[4] C. Wordsworth: *Salisbury Processions and Ceremonies* (1901), p. 171 (Item corona una argent'. cum cathenis iii argent. cum columba argent'. ad eukaristiam).

[5] The altar-screen of French stone, known as the Neville Screen.

that the pyx did hang on, was of gold, and the cords that did draw it up and down was made of fine white strong silk.'[1]

As the foregoing description indicates, the pyx was covered by a cloth, in this instance of lawn. But in other examples the pyx hung under a fringed canopy which was cone-shaped. Such an example is the pyx-cloth belonging to Hessett Church, Suffolk.[2] (See Plate 23.) In other instances the pyx was suspended inside a triple-crown or tiara. A celebrated example is depicted in the Islip Roll belonging to Westminster Abbey, made about 1532.[3] In this case the tiara hung from the tester which was projected over the High altar at Westminster.

A form of hanging pyx which caught the imagination of the antiquarians of the nineteenth century was that in the shape of a dove; so much was this the case that some of the Eucharistic doves that now repose in museums are believed to be fakes of the last century. Nevertheless there can be no doubt that this form of hanging pyx was widely used in France (see Plate 24), and this custom prevailed in that country in some places down to the nineteenth century. Bossuet, the celebrated Bishop of Meaux (d. 1704), in his treatise, *Défense de la tradition sur la communion sous une espèce* (2e partie, chap. xix), says: 'L'Eucharistie, que le Saint Espirit, figuré par la colombe, consecre, d'ou le Saint Espirit se répand pour vivifier les âmes et les corps.' But such doves were also used in baptistries for containing the oil of anointing in the Latin rite of Baptism. Likewise there are examples of reliquaries of this form. Such a reliquary was suspended over the tomb of St. Denis, Paris.[4]

St. Thomas Aquinas received from Pope Urban IV (d. 1264) a silver dove upon his completion of the work of composing the Office for the Feast of Corpus Christi.[5]

As we have already remarked that while the hanging pyx was the usual form of reservation in England prior to 1549, such a pyx was not usually in the form of a dove. But only in the Marian reaction and restoration of 1553 was the standing tabernacle for the reservation of the Blessed Sacrament on the altar introduced in some places by Cardinal Pole.[6]

[1] *The Rites of Durham*, written in 1593 (Surtees Soc. Vol. 107 (1903), p. 8).
[2] For other examples, see F. Bond: *The Chancel of English Churches*, pp. 24–6.
[3] See J. Perkins: *Westminster Abbey* (1938), Vol. 1, illustration facing p. 50.
[4] E. Maffei: *La Réservation Eucharistique* (Brussels, 1942), p. 31.
[5] *Revue de L'Art Chrétien*, 1858, p. 393.
[6] Wilkins: *Concilia*, iv, 157.

The late W. H. Freestone stated: 'In Italy and Spain suspension seems never to have been usual.'[1] This statement appears to have been accepted and expanded by the late Dom Gregory Dix,[2] who inferred that the method of reservation by suspension was peculiar to the northern temperament. Our readers will see under Plate 25 an example of a hanging pyx in the form of a spire-like structure from a manuscript made for King James II of Majorca in 1337. As regards Italy Braun illustrates more than one example of a hanging pyx now to be seen in the museums of that land, although not all of these may have originated in Italy.[3] More than one commentator has, however, drawn attention to Italian ciboria which have hooks from which the Eucharistic pyx must have hung. Such appears to be the case in the churches of St. Agnes and St. Clement, Rome, and St. Mary in Trastevere.[4] The Cathedral at Salzburg, Austria, has one of the most handsome examples of a Eucharistic Dove (see Plate 26), thereby showing that the hanging pyx was not unknown in Central Europe. The idea, therefore, that this form of reservation was peculiar to Northern Europe is myth, which Dix failed to detect in his pursuit of certain presuppositions regarding the use of the aumbry as a method of reserving the Blessed Sacrament.

It should be made clear that only since the seventeenth century and the era of the Counter Reformation has the Roman Catholic Church insisted on a rigid uniformity in regard to the method and place of reserving the Blessed Sacrament in a parish church. The hanging pyx, the wall aumbry, the Sacrament house standing on a column were all recognized as suitable methods of reservation in the late middle ages.[5] Indeed, some of these methods were continued until the nineteenth century in various parts of Europe.

Since the second half of the last century under the influence of the Oxford Movement perpetual reservation of the Holy Sacrament has become an accepted custom in the Church of England. From 1928 the wall aumbry on account of its practical convenience has been widely adopted; and has now been officially sanctioned by most diocesan chancellors. But it would be incorrect to assume that the hanging pyx may no longer be employed, since this method of reservation was introduced in Gloucester Cathedral by the Dean and Chapter

[1] Freestone: op. cit., p. 195.
[2] G. Dix: *A Detection of Aumbries* (1942), pp. 42–3.
[3] Braun: op. cit., Vol. 2, Plates 352–4.
[4] J. A. Martigny: *Dictionnaire des antiquities chrétiennes* (2nd ed., Paris, 1877), p. 189.
[5] E. Maffei: op. cit., pp. 23–123; also Braun: Vol. II, pp. 586 ff.

in 1958. More recently the Royal Foundation of St. Katherine, London, had a pyx hung over the High altar; while in the Southwark diocese a faculty was granted by the Bishop and his Chancellor in 1961 for this method of reservation in the Parish Church of St. Nicholas, Plumstead.[1] The assumption sometimes made that this method of reserving the Blessed Sacrament is illegal can no longer be seriously entertained.

[1] Faculties for hanging pyxes have also been granted at Newport Pagnell and Stony Stratford in the Oxford Diocese.

7

Some Practical Considerations in the Design of an Altar

(1) THERE is no rule, Anglican or Roman, requiring the High altar to be mounted on *three* steps. Much will depend on the size of the sanctuary. Space rather than additional steps should be the primary consideration. The foot-pace on which the altar stands should not be more than 2 feet 9 inches from the front of the altar to the edge of the step, and not less than 2 feet 6 inches.

(2) The riser of any step should not be more than 6 inches, and 5 inches is preferable. Subsidiary steps below the foot-pace are frequently too narrow. Their width should not be less than 22 inches and 25 inches is preferable. Where space allows they should be carried right across the sanctuary rather than returned each side.

(3) If the altar is of stone it should have one slab on top; and it should be one piece of natural stone or marble, not concrete or any artificial composition. The front of the altar should not have detailed carving on it, nor should it be decorated and gilded, so that on the last three days of Holy Week when it is exposed it does not present a festive appearance.

Wooden altars should also be free of unnecessary carving and decoration.

(4) The height of an altar should be 3 feet 3 inches, and not more than 3 feet 5 inches; and it must be wide enough to take a corporal of twenty inches square. It can be wider, but if it is made wider than 3 feet 6 inches there will be difficulties about vesting and clothing the table. The top of the altar should project two or three inches on the side on which the celebrant stands to give room for his feet.

(5) Altars should always stand clear of a wall or reredos. This is important for the cleanliness and vesting of the altar. Gradines or shelves are now going out of use everywhere and this is to be commended.

(6) Where the conventional type of altar frontal is in use this should not be mounted on a wooden frame, but suspended from an aluminium

or copper tube (steel tubing rusts), which is supported by lugs or hooks under the front of the altar. There should be two 'frontals' where the altar is visible on both sides. If not, the 'throw-over' type of cloth should be used. Over the top of the altar hangs the frontlet (incorrectly called the 'super-frontal'). This should not be more than six inches in depth and it should be attached to the coarse linen cloth which covers the top of the altar and hangs some inches down the back. At the back of this cloth there should be an open seam through which a rod may hang to help keep the frontlet and its cloth in position.

(7) Altars which have oil or chrism used at their consecration require a wax or cere-cloth to prevent the oil from soiling the fair linen. The fair linen should not merely cover the top of the altar, but hang right down each side to the foot-pace. Nothing is more mean and contrary to the spirit of sound liturgical practice than a fair linen cloth which only hangs a few inches over the ends of the altar. Lace and crochet are to be avoided on fair linen. They are the product of the less virile ages of liturgical worship and were quite unknown in the primitive and early medieval period.

(8) The canopy, tester or baldaquin should not only cover the area of the altar, but also that of the foot-pace. It will, therefore, be four-square and not oblong in plan.

APPENDIX

WE have alluded to the orientation, the occidentation and the general alignment of the great Roman basilicas (pp. 88–100 *passim*). Several commentators have stressed that the orientation of church buildings was more strictly observed in the countries north of the Alps and that in Italy the alignment of the building was treated with indifference. A statement of this nature is imprecise and needs more careful qualification.

Our observations made on visits to Italy show that outside Rome many of the older churches were orientated, that is, they had an axis running from west to east, with the altar at the east end. Amongst such churches we have noted the following:

Milan: the Cathedral, the Basilica of St. Ambrose (*Sant' Ambrogio*); Pisa: the Cathedral, San Michele in Borgo; Florence: the Cathedral, Santa Croce; Rome: San Petronilla in the catacombs of Domitilla; Ravenna: Sant' Apollinare in Classe, Sant' Apollinare Nuovo; Venice: the Cathedral (*San Marco*), San Zaccaria, St. John and St. Paul (*S. Zanipolo*); Ferrara: the Cathedral; Padua: Basilica of St. Anthony, Santa Giustina; Siena: the Cathedral.

It is in the period of the Renaissance and later that the traditional orientation of churches on new sites came to be ignored or abandoned, as we can note in the example of Santa Maria della Salute, Venice, designed by Longhena in 1631, which has an alignment from north to south, with the altar at the southern end. The Baroque church of the Immaculate Conception, Turin, by Guarini, finished in 1697, reveals a similar disregard for orientation. On the other hand, churches rebuilt in the Renaissance and Baroque periods usually retained the axis or alignment of the older one which had stood on the site. Thus San Giorgio Maggiore, Venice, rebuilt by Palladio in 1610 on the site of an older church, has an alignment from west to east.

SELECT BIBLIOGRAPHY

M. Andrieu: *Les Ordines Romani du Haut Moyen Age*, 5 vols. (Louvain, 1931–61).

M. Andrieu: *Le Pontifical Romain au Moyen Age*, 4 vols., Rome (1938–41).

F. Bond: *Introduction to English Church Architecture*, 2 vols. (1913).

F. Bond: *The Chancel of English Churches* (1916).

E. Bishop: *Liturgica Historica* (1918), article, The Christian Altar.

J. Braun: *Der christliche Altar in seiner geistlichen Entwicklung*, 2 vols. (Munich, 1924).

F. Cabrol and H. Leclercq: *Dictionnaire d'Archéologie Chrétienne et de Liturgie*, 15 vols. (Paris, 1907–1953). Quoted as D.A.C.L.

J. N. Comper: *Further Thoughts on the English Altar, or Practical Considerations on the Planning of a Modern Church* (1933).

Corpus Scriptorum Ecclesiasticorum Latinorum (Vienna, 1866, et seqq.), quoted as C.S.E.L.

D. R. Dendy: *The Use of Lights in Christian Worship* (1959).

L. Duchesne: *Christian Worship: Its Origins and Evolution* (5th ed., 1919).

L. Duchesne: *Le Liber Pontificalis*, 2 vols. (Paris, 1886–92).

Walter Howard Frere: A collection of His Papers on Liturgical and Historical Subjects, Ed. J. H. Arnold and E. G. P. Wyatt (Alcuin Club Collections, XXV, 1940).

J. A. Jungmann: *The Early Liturgy* (London, 1960).

J. A. Jungmann: *The Mass of the Roman Rite*, 2 vols. (New York, 1951–55).

F. Van der Meer and Christine Mohrmann: *Atlas of the Early Christian World* (1958).

J. P. Migne: *Patrologia Graeca* (Paris, 1844, et seqq.), quoted as P.G.

J. P. Migne: *Patrologia Latina* (Paris, 1844, et seqq.), quoted as P.L.

J. D. Mansi: *Sacrorum Conciliorum nova et amplissima Collectio*, 31 vols. (Florence, 1759–98), quoted as Mansi.

R. W. Muncey: *A History of the Consecration of Churches and Churchyards* (1930).

C. E. Pocknee: *Liturgical Vesture, its origins and development* (1960).

C. E. Pocknee: *Cross and Crucifix in Christian Worship and Devotion* (1962).

D. Rock: *The Church of our Fathers*, new edition, 4 vols. C. W. Hart and W. H. Frere (1905).

S. Salaville: *An Introduction to the study of Eastern Liturgies*, translated from the French by J. M. T. Barton (1938).

D. Stone: *A History of the Holy Eucharist*, 2 vols., 1909.

W. H. Freestone: *The Sacrament Reserved* (1917), Alcuin Club Collections XXI.

S. J. P. van Dijk and J. H. Walker: *The Myth of the Aumbry* (1957).

E. Maffei: *La resérvation eucharistique jusqu'à la Renaissance* (Brussels, 1942).

F. C. N. Hicks: *The Fullness of Sacrifice* (2nd ed.) 1938.

F. Wieland: *Mensa und Confessio* (Munich, 1906).

F. Wieland: *Altar und Altargrab der Christlichen Kirchen im 4 Jahrhundert* (Munich, 1912).

INDEX

Altar Cloths, 46, 107
Altar Cross, 13, 41, 49
Altare, 13, 35-6, 42
Altars without relics, 39-41
Ambrose, 21, 39, 99
Antependium, 46
Antimension, 45
Ara, 35
Augustine of Canterbury, 56
Augustine of Hippo, 36, 90

Baldachino or Baldaquin, 58
Benedictional, 57
Brandea, 39
Burchard, 49

Candlesticks, 13, 41, 50
Chrysostom, 45, 55
Ciborium or Ciboria, 19, 55-9, 107
Churches:
  Anagni Cathedral, 18, 61
  Athens Cathedral, 97
  Auxerre Cathedral, 58
  Besançon Cathedral, 38
  Canterbury Cathedral, 94
  Carthage, 95
  Castel Sant' Elia, 17, 56, 61, 93
  Chichester Cathedral, 52, 85
  Chipping Campden, 46
  Clun, Salop, 27, 57
  Coventry Cathedral, 15
  Croyland Abbey, 47
  Durham Cathedral, 102
  El Asaba, 82
  Ely Cathedral, 41
  Gerona Cathedral, 23, 58
  Grado, Santa Maria, 81
  Hessett, Suffolk, 71, 103
  Holy Wisdom, Constantinople, 29, 56, 100
  Hopperstad, Norway, 27
  Il Gesú, Rome, 65, 85
  Lincoln Cathedral, 59, 102
  Ludlow Priory, 57
  Mainz Cathedral, 96
  Norwich Cathedral, 66, 95
  St. Agnes, Rome, 104
  St. Albans Abbey, 47, 85
  St. Ambrose, Milan, 21, 39, 46, 56
  St. Andrew, Aberdeen, 80
  St. Andrew, Rome, 56
  Sant' Apollinare in Classe, 19, 45, 56, 87

  Sant' Apollinare Nuovo, 81
  San Clemente in Cassauria, 61
  San Clemente, Rome, 56, 81, 104
  St. Gall, Switzerland, 96
  St. John Hungate, 37
  St. John Lateran, 37, 56, 87, 92
  St. Lawrence, Rome, 56, 93
  Santa Maria in Cosmedin, 56, 81
  St. Martin, Rome, 56
  St. Mary Major, 92
  St. Mary in Trastevere, 104
  St. Mary, Wellingborough, 59
  St. Mary Woolnoth, 26, 59
  St. Paul's Cathedral, London, 15, 85, 98
  St. Paul's outside-the-walls, 92
  St. Peter, Rome, 28, 38, 64, 90, 92
  San Vitale, Ravenna, 45, 100
  Salisbury Cathedral, 44, 102
  Salzburg Cathedral, 74
  Tewkesbury Abbey, 41
  Theveste, 82
  Terracina Cathedral, 61, 76, 95
  Torcello Cathedral, 81
  Westminster Abbey, 24, 53, 57, 85
  Winchester Cathedral, 53
Confessio, 17, 18, 38, 92
Consecration of altars, 42-3
Constantine the Great, 45, 55
Cyprian, 36
Cyril of Jerusalem, 99

Durandus, 96

Endyton or *ependysis*, 47
Ethelwold, 57
Eucharistic Dove, 74, 102
Eusebius, 64

Fenestella, 17
Flowers and flower vases, 14, 42
Fortunatianus, 36
Frontals, 14, 46, 106

Gregory of Nazianzus, 36
Guilds, 53

Iconostasis, 29, 69, 82-3
Ignatius of Antioch, 34, 51

Jerome, 99

Lactantius, 36
Liturgical Colours, 48
Lyndwood, 40, 102

Martyrium, 38
Mensa, 13, 42
Minucius Felix, 36

Occidentation, 92, 96
Optatus, 45
Ordines Romani, 61, 93
Orientation, 13, 88–99
Origen, 36, 45

Palla Corporalis, 46
Perpetua, 95
Pontificals:
　Alet, 61
　Durandus, 57
　Egbert, 61
　Magdalen, 57
　Roman, 47
　Romano-Germanic, 96
　York, 40
Popes:
　Gregory the Great, 51
　Innocent III, 48
　John VI, 61
　Leo the Great, 90
　Leo III, 61
　Pelagius II, 38

Sergius, 61
Sylvester, 37
Vigilius, 96
Prayer to the East, 88–92
Pyx, 101–5

Relics, 39–41, 84
Reliquaries, 31, 49, 84
Reredos, 19, 23, 86
Roman Missal, 41, 47, 77, 99

Screens before the Altar, 29, 81–3
Screens behind the Altar, 83–7
Sepulcrum, 39
Side Altars, 51–4
Stone Altars, 15, 37–9, 42
Super-altars, 20, 43–4

Tertullian, 35, 90
Tester, 22, 27, 57
Θυσία, 35
Θυσιαστήριον, 13, 33–6, 42
Τράπεζα, 13, 33, 42
Triptych, 30, 68, 86

Veils, 59–63

Willigis, 96
Wooden Altars, 36–7
Wooden super-altars, 44